A HANDELIAN'S NOTEBOOK

William C. Smith

D1486649

LONDON

ADAM & CHARLES BLACK

FIRST PUBLISHED 1965
By A. AND C. BLACK LIMITED
4, 5 AND 6 SOHO SQUARE, LONDON W.1

CONTENTS

To
Gerald Coke

fellow Handelian
and very good friend

PREFACE

THIS IS A personal story, but it has particular reference to Handel, and as such is a gathering together of information about the composer and his works, collectors and collections of them, exhibitions, performances, editors and other interesting general and personal material. It is not, except in the earlier part, a connected narrative, but a miscellaneous collection of notes, transcriptions, reports and comments, some of which are not generally known or easily accessible; some are new and others worthwhile recording in this form as they might otherwise be forgotten.

One aspect of the subject has been borne in mind – the need to bring to notice particulars of Handelian sources and authorities that may help in further studies of the composer and his works. The material is roughly grouped where possible, and the Indexes make reference to the work quite easy.

Special attention is given to the stage and concert performances of the operas and stage productions of the oratorios in my time, a subject which is of increasing interest to-day and the records of which are scattered about in press notices, private papers and programmes.

While the ground covered is mainly the English scene, the latter part of the book gives a brief survey of what was done in Germany from the 1920's up to the end of the 1939–45 war to re-establish Handel as a major composer, particularly in the field of Opera. The post war period, not dealt with here except for some brief references to the Handel Festivals at Halle and Göttingen will, I hope, be the subject of a future work.

The selections, quotations and notes are such as seem to me to be especially worth recording, but represent only a few of the publications that could have been quoted. Many more musicians and authors than those named have contributed to my enjoyment

9

of Handel's music and helped me to understand and appreciate the life, work and personality of the composer.

This is a tribute to all those to whom I am indebted in any way, and an apology to any who feel that they should have been mentioned or whose work I may have misrepresented. My grateful thanks are especially due to Norman Stone who has been particularly helpful, and to all those who have so freely given me permission to quote from their works.

I

EARLY YEARS AT THE
BRITISH MUSEUM

WHEN I WAS APPOINTED to the staff of the British Museum in September, 1900, I had no idea that my professional and private life would be henceforth closely asociated with music; that I should become an enthusiastic Handelian, and that as such I should in later years be a frequent visitor to Handel Festivals at Halle, the composer's birthplace behind the Iron Curtain, where I would see and hear much about the social and political conditions in Communist dominated East Germany.

I had previously visited the British Museum once or twice, but that behind its public galleries there was one of the greatest libraries in the world, including the finest music collection in the Commonwealth, was unknown to me, as to many of the everyday visitors.

Two years before – in 1898 – I had passed into the temporary grade of the Civil Service, which terminated at twenty, and in this capacity had served two years in the Inland Revenue Department at Somerset House.

In those days there were two main grades of the Civil Service, the First and the Second Divisions. The former was quite out of my reach, demanding a university degree or education of that standing; but the second was open to lads who, like myself, had a reasonable mental equipment and who could assimilate enough of the essential subjects in a two or three years cramming course at evening classes held at King's College, London, and elsewhere. The competition at the examinations was very keen, and as the number of successful candidates depended entirely on the demands of the various departments at the time, the Civil Service Commissioners announced the number of vacancies for each of the examinations. From memory, the number of entrants at the particular Second Division examination that I passed in 1900 was over eleven hundred – and the vacancies eighty (afterwards increased considerably).

I suppose I was really fortunate in having a good memory, but I had no particular ability at arithmetic or allied subjects. History and geography had always interested me, I could always write a reasonable hand, and orthography and composition were not a trial. At any rate, to my surprise, I passed – due partly to one or two fortuitous circumstances. One was the kindness of the head of the department in which I was employed at Somerset House. O'Connor was his name. We juniors had a certain amount of work to do every day. When that was finished, we were encouraged to get down to our studies, and very often one or other of us was allowed to leave before the official day was over. I have never forgotten the wise and helpful example of Mr. O'Connor in dealing with his subordinate staff, many of whom duly passed into a permanent position in the Service. I also had some extraordinarily good luck before the examination in having looked up one or two knotty problems that duly appeared in the questions. One in particular was to draw a map of the northern hemisphere with the North Pole as centre, showing the quickest route round the world; another, to draw a map of the railways, existing or projected, in Africa. As I had just studied the route of the Trans-Siberian Railway, then recently opened, and also the projected Cape to Cairo Railway, I did extremely well in geography – shall I say by a happy accident?

Thus for the first time in my early life, which had always been overshadowed by the financial uncertainty of my father's business, I felt a measure of security in a permanent government appointment, a position not then so common as it is to-day. To be a "Civil Servant", of whatever grade, was a distinction, and I could not help feeling a certain pride although it was tempered with a little anxiety as to the type of work I should be expected to do. My two years in the Inland Revenue had made it clear that the permanent clerks in that department lived lives of dull and over-powering routine, and I felt quite unable to accept with en-thusiasm that kind of career for myself. However, the fates were kind. After some six months in the Scottish Education Depart-ment (to which I was appointed in a temporary capacity) my official life was spent in the British Museum – of which more in due course.

The Scottish Education Department, then as now, had its London offices in a fine historic house with an entrance in Whitehall, and with rooms looking on to the Horse Guards Parade at the back. It was formerly the home of the first Lord Melbourne, and was afterwards known as York House and Dover House, still retaining in my time much of its early attractive in-terior style.

The Principal was Sir Henry Craik, and his chief of the ad-ministrative staff a Mr. ———, who had probably risen from the lower rungs of the official ladder to his position of control. He appeared to me (the little I saw of him) as a man of limited culture and intellect, but much pomposity and power. I may be wrong; but he provoked in me a strong antipathy to that sort of person being in charge of others. His subordinates, with few exceptions, were spineless and obsequious, and appeared to tremble and lose the power to act on their own initiative when Sir Henry was in, or Mr. ——— wanted to see them.

My work, even making allowances for the fact that I was a junior, was of the dullest; and I remember that in my spare moments I tried to get some relief by studying the office copy of *Whitaker's Almanack* – not an uninteresting work by any means, but limited in its appeal to the emotions or imagination. The rather pleasant room, overlooking the Horse Guards Parade, where I worked, was overcrowded, and when my term of temporary em-ployment was over I left the department with no regret, hoping that the Civil Service Commission would send me to nothing worse. Much to my surprise I was told to report to the British Museum, one of the last places in which I should have expected to find myself.

On September 3, 1900 I duly presented myself at the Director's office. A small, pale, rather nervous and uncertain youngster, with the typical bowler hat, gloves and stick so usual at the time, I had, nevertheless, tucked away somewhere in my make-up a feeling of determination, and a little hope that I was on the way to a career at last.

I cannot pretend to describe adequately the great personalities who administered the various departments of the Museum, or to give a convincing picture of the character, charm and dignity of the interior of the building which, since those days, has suffered so much from the various schemes of reconstruction and modification – some of which were not carried out to their intended completion, and which, although they may have helped to satisfy the demands for more space and equipment, have certainly taken away from the Department of Printed Books some of its old architectural beauty and restfulness.

The Director was Sir Edward Maunde Thompson, widely known as a scholar – and by many of the Museum staff feared as a martinet. I must plead little personal knowledge of him, but the few interviews that I had with him showed him to be courteous if rather austere.

After being received by the Secretary of the Museum I was conducted through the impressive public galleries of manuscripts and printed books to Dr. G. K. Fortescue, the Keeper of Printed Books, who received me with the grace, kindness and charm so characteristic of that fine scholar, who was remembered with affection by his staff long after he had passed away.

Fortescue enquired about my qualifications and, for some reason not clear to me at the time, asked whether I was musical. From my very limited experiences as a bad pianist and worse violinist I was able to say quite truthfully: "Oh, yes! I play the violin and piano." To which Fortescue replied: "Excellent, you're just the man we want!" And without further explanation I was taken round to a member of the staff – John Macfarlane – and placed under his tuition to learn something of the intricate business of cataloguing printed books.

In those days the King's Library (damaged during the 1939–45 war, and subsequently restored and redecorated) was the same imposing gallery as it is to-day, with, throughout its length, showcases containing famous examples of early printed books, etc. At the North end, as at present, there was a door leading to the working rooms of the Department of Printed Books, which gave a different impression to one than do the reconstructed rooms of to-day. At that time, after entering the Catalogue Room, if the fine double doors were opened up, you could look through five other magnificent rooms along the whole north side of the Museum to the extreme end of the Arched Room, which terminated in a high window (still existing) looking on to the gardens of the houses in Gower Street. These rooms were all very lofty, and were divided on each side into a series of recesses by built-out double-sided shelves, finished off at each end with glazed cases for show pieces and especially valuable books. The next room to the Catalogue Room was the Music Room, where I was destined to spend much of my time until 1922. The third room, which was larger than the others and which was also approached directly from the main Reading Room, was known as the Large Room or the North Library. It was used by readers of special or valuable works. This room to-day has little similarity to its forerunner, having been twice reconstructed since my early days. Now, the one time pleasing vista through the whole range of rooms is impossible. Four of the rooms have been entirely changed in style by having extra floors of iron and concrete put in them, and all available space filled with steel shelving – characterless and with various technical faults that make some of them unsuitable, and most difficult of access.

Admitting the ever growing need for increased space to house the enormous quantity of literature being turned out year by year, no one who is really familiar with the story of the development of the department can feel happy at the hotchpotch arrangements and working conditions provided from time to time in many parts of this famous library so essential to many aspirants to fame in the literary and bibliographical world.

The Reading Room was very much as it is to-day except for decoration and furnishings. In 1907 it was redecorated, including the painting of the names of nineteen great English writers in the panels below the windows. These names were much criticized at the time, some critics pointing out the absence of the name of any woman writer, and many disagreeing about the relative merits of those chosen for these places of honour in such a famous centre of literature. The names were removed some years later, and in 1952 the Room was redecorated and the roof repaired where it had been damaged by bombs in the 1939–45 war, and it was redecorated again in 1963–64. From time to time improvements have been made in the fitments and lighting, and the original ironwork galleries outside the Room have been partially reconstructed and filled up with closepacked steel shelving. Unfortunately the result of inserting this steel shelving has been that the books in some cases cannot be seen without artificial lighting, and owing to the size of the shelves the old order of press placing and arrangement has been given up.

The administrative and higher grade of the staff (known as Assistants, Deputy Keepers and Keeper) were comparatively few in number, and because of the size of the rooms and the ample accommodation, each individual seemed set apart, almost as a single figure on a big stage. The nature of the work entailed a great deal of movement from one's desk to the Catalogue Room and other parts of the library, through the great rooms, in each of which only one or two people were employed. There was no hurry. Everybody moved about quietly and, as it semed to me, with dignity and self-restraint. There was an old-world air, not only about the place but about the manners of the staff. I was kindly reminded in my first week that in the British Museum one did not place a pen behind the ear – it was not done! The distance between the desks precluded any intimate conversation unless you made it your business to go and talk to someone.

The most significant superficial difference in the staff between then and now was in the matter of dress. The silk hat, morning-coat or frock-coat, with the usual accessories of white shirts and stiff collars, were the general order of the day; and if one could not affect these, nothing less than dark lounge suits and bowler hats was expected. Such a thing as a soft felt hat was not seen in the department until well on in the century, and however hot and stuffy the atmosphere, no one dared to appear in shirt sleeves except in the washing rooms.

These were only some of the minor things that made me realize I had entered a new world, peopled as it seemed to me by well-to-do folk of surprising attainments, and with illimitable knowledge. And comparatively I was not altogether wrong, for the assistant staff at that time consisted in the main of men who were not only eminent for their official work, but who were known for their research, publications and activities outside the Museum, G. K. Fortescue, A. W. K. Miller, G. F. Barwick, Nisbet Bain, Robert Proctor, W. Barclay Squire, A. W. Pollard, Richard Streatfeild, George Calderon, John Macfarlane, John A. J. de Villiers and Cyril Davenport. They were great figures – representative of a tradition and of a period which it is easy enough to discount – who had as high, if not higher, standards of qualifications, service and output than some of them are given credit for to-day. I wonder whether so great a proportion of the present day upper staff of the department compared with those of a generation or so ago will be so well remembered as personalities, or their names so widely known outside of the Museum, thirty or forty years after they have passed on. I could qualify this by naming some present and recent members of the staff who will be exceptions in this respect, and the flowering of others may come later and add to the number of those who will achieve a reputation for personal and individual literary, bibliographical and other research work. In these days so many more are in the Museum (as in other Civil Service departments) for a career – the choice of which is not governed by their tastes as it more often was in my early days, when the entrants to the senior grades were not entirely without some private means.

I clearly remember how different I appeared to be in knowledge, culture and ability to the giants around me, and how unattainable seemed the exalted world in which they thought and moved. In the words of Kenneth Grahame dare I ask the question to-day: "Can it be that I also have become an Olympian?"

So far I have spoken only of the upper staff of the Department. To use the current words of the time, there was a subordinate

2

grade – Attendants – whose duty it was, in the main, to fetch and carry for the Readers, and for the Assistants. Recruited without much regard to education, but carefully chosen largely from the families of servants of the Trustees, or other well-to-do people, the attendants as a class were distinct and exceptional. Most of them, very carefully dressed, endeavoured to carry themselves with a dignity of fussy importance intended to convey that they were not as other folk. As many of them had grown up familiar with domestic service, they seemed to bear the marks of their origins (worthy as they were) in the immaculate polish on their boots and a punctilious regard for their clothes. Some of them had grace and charm, and they were by no means all without knowledge of other than the three R's. I believe that the ultimate salary of most of them was £120 per annum after many years of service, and to supplement this they did various jobs in their evenings or on off days. Waiting at restaurants and social functions, ushering of sorts at theatres and elsewhere, and other similar work came their way. They would be found as extras in the refreshment tents at the Eton and Harrow and other cricket matches, in the ornamental uniform of attendants at the Royal Opera, Covent Garden, or even occasionally as footmen complete with livery, riding high through the London streets behind the carriage of some distinguished person in a civic or other public procession. Most of them brought their midday meal to the Museum in the popular black gladstone bag affected in those days, and after a day's or evening's waiting at table were able to produce some "perks" for a cold collation next day at the Museum in the shape of a portion of chicken or game and a bottle of wine. Some kept small boarding houses. I remember many of them with pleasure for their kindness and courtesy to me; and I could tell many good stories about them, but two must suffice.

At one time a Keeper who was given to irascibility if interrupted, had as attendant a dear delightful fellow who knew his job outside the Keeper's room and how to deal with his chief's moments of annoyance. A visitor arrived with a book to sell. The attendant, who had naturally acquired some knowledge of bibliography and sale items, turned the leaves over disparagingly in front of the owner, then entered the Keeper's room. The attendant: "There's a man with a ..." The Keeper: "Damn you – get outside!" The attendant (withdrawing): "Shall I say ten shillings, Sir?"

Many years later one attendant, who had carried on a successful bookmaking business, decided to retire. His chief did not want to lose him, so he sent for him and asked him why he wanted to leave, saying that he was very useful and asking could he afford it. The attendant replied to the effect that he had always been wanted if there was some work to be done, but not when there were any promotions about, and that he was going! Said his chief: "But what are you going to do?" "Going round the world", said the attendant, financially covered no doubt by his successful bookmaking activities which were unknown to his chief.

The Second Division grade in the Civil Service was not generally employed in the specialist departments of the Museum until about a year before my entrance. One or two of them were, however, appointed to the Secretary's office some fifteen years or so earlier. It had been a problem in the Department of Printed Books for some time to find a method of increasing the staff employed on cataloguing, without adding to the number of assistants. This difficulty was overcome by appointing a few members of the Second Division grade – of which I was the second recruit. A few more were added between then and the First World War, after which recruitment ceased. Two of the then existing members of the grade were subsequently promoted to Assistantships – of which I was one – and the others were transferred to other Public Service departments.

It is unnecessary to enter here into the long arguments and discussions which took place during the reorganization of the Museum staff after the 1914–18 War as to what should be done with the Second Division men. The comparatively poor prospects for assistants, and their low range of salaries, precluded the lower grade from doing as well as they expected to do in the larger departments outside the Museum, and this made them justly dissatisfied. I myself seriously thought of applying for a transfer, but I decided to remain and gamble on the chance of succeeding my eminent chief, W. Barclay Squire, of whom more presently.

Looking back now, I feel that on the whole I made a wise decision – again the Fates were kind. With Squire's backing, (of which I knew little at the time) I succeeded him in 1920, and thus had an opportunity for more specialization in all branches of musical librarianship and research, in addition to the advantage of having the Music Department of the Library under my own control – subject to the authority of the Keeper of Printed Books. I was also promoted to the Assistant grade, afterwards known as Assistant Keepers.

At the Museum I was employed at first on cataloguing copyright books for six months or so – work which, if limited in scope, provided me with the opportunity to come into contact with much literature of which I was quite ignorant. Then my occupation was suddenly changed. W. Barclay Squire, Assistant in charge of the Printed Music since 1885, was well known as a scholar, musicologist, musical critic and writer. Associating with many of the musicians and literary people of the day, he lived an active life, and was able to keep up a standard of comfort and artistic enjoyment above that of some of his colleagues – being a bachelor with a nice house in Kensington and some private means. He was always immaculately dressed, and had a fine person and dignified appearance – which are clearly recorded in William Strang's drawing of him reproduced in *The Musical Times* of February 1, 1908, and an engraving of which hangs in the Music Department to-day.

Squire was at heart a kindly and helpful soul, but somehow, except to his intimates, seemed austere, reserved and unemotional. A certain diffidence and anxiety not to intrude on others not of his immediate circle may explain what appeared to be indifference. I worked with him from 1901 until his retirement in 1920, and during the whole of that time our relationships were without discord or even a minor disagreement; but I never felt that I knew him or that he knew me. He did me many kind actions and although he rarely commented on my work, obviously appreciated it, for he allowed me to assume more and more of the work of the department, whilst he specialized particularly on his *Catalogue of Printed Music published between 1487 and 1800 now in the British Museum*. The fact that he left me entirely alone officially to acquire knowledge of the department, and gave me ample opportunities to do all kinds of work within my attainments are things for which I have always been grateful to him.

In the first six months of my service in the Museum I hardly spoke to Squire, except to say "Good morning" or "Good day" – there seemed no chance of getting nearer to him than that. Then one morning he came along to my desk with a pile of sheet music in his arms, which he plumped down in front of me, saying: "The Keeper says you can help me. Here are some songs to be catalogued – you will find out how to do them by consulting the catalogue. If there is anything you don't know, ask me." They were the first and almost the only instructions I ever got from Squire, and the incident explained to me in a flash the cryptic remarks of Dr. Fortescue six months earlier, as to whether I was musical, and that I was the man they wanted. What a good job for me that neither Fortescue nor Squire knew the depths of my ignorance about the history, theory and practice of music!

Personally, I was not pleased at being switched from books to music. I could get some interest out of the contents of the books I was cataloguing, but sheet music I could not appreciate, and the cataloguing of it except for the technical problems involved was exceedingly uninteresting. However, it was too early in my career to complain, and I faced up to the job and soon became an efficient cataloguer of every kind of music – English and foreign, and Squire soon left the whole of that side of the department to me; only checking my work when it was in proof.

I soon realized my educational limitations, not only in the field of music, but generally; and I set about trying to make up for my ignorance. I read widely, joined various classes at King's College and elsewhere for instruction in Italian and other subjects, and endeavoured to acquire some better knowledge of French, German and Latin, in which I had had some instruction at my last school. I was attracted, bewildered and encouraged by the miles of books around me, and as up to this time I had read along

no particular lines I saw the importance of some organized plan
of making up for my lack of knowledge. But I soon found out
that reading could mean much more than that, and that the pleasure derived from the form and style of a work often meant more
than the subject matter.

Looking back to those years of the early 'twenties I cannot
remember how it was that I became interested in this or that
writer – perhaps this is true of most more or less self-cultured
people who have not had the benefits or experience of educational
direction after school years. I expect I just blundered into things –
partly no doubt as the result of what had gone before to the
making of my personality in the circumstances of my home
and social life. But what did it matter where the urge came from
– I loved books – and reading meant to me "the gateway to all
knowledge", as Ruskin said. Later on I began to read on some
definite lines – theology and comparative religion, social and
industrial history, the art, development and appreciation of
music (stimulated by my work in the Music Department of the
Museum), poetry and dramatic literature; although in the main
I found myself dipping into any book that took my fancy by
the way.

In my early years at the Museum it was possible for members
of the staff to pick up through the Keeper and others all sorts of
research and copying jobs, which were done in one's own time
and privately paid for. In this respect I was exceptionally fortunate,
as Squire placed much work of this kind in my way, particularly
in connection with music, musical history and biography – the
earnings from which, at a shilling or two an hour, were of great
advantage to me as a supplement to my modest income, which
was only just over two pounds a week when I married in 1907.

Among the private jobs I did was much music copying, in
those days all done by hand, as it was before the present-day
methods of photostating and microfilming; a bibliography of
personal travels in Sicily; the references to Miss Willmott's
standard work on roses; much research work for Fuller-
Maitland, the Comte de St. Foix, Sir Arthur Somervell and
others; work on the first catalogue of the Times Book Club; and

a catalogue of Sir Henry Wood's library. I even attempted, at Squire's suggestion, the preparation of a record of *The Italian Opera and Contemporary Ballet in London, 1789–1820* – a work which remained unpublished until it appeared under the auspices of the Theatre Research Society in 1955.

When I married in September 1907, I suppose I was taking a risk of financial embarrassment that would make married life a strain and burden, but I thought that I knew what I was doing, and my fiancée was quite prepared for the adventure. I said nothing at the Museum about my intention except to one or two intimate colleagues of the Second Division grade, and to Barclay Squire. The former, being used to the same financial limitations as I was, saw nothing exceptional in marriage on a small salary; and Barclay Squire, too much of a gentleman to make personal comments, preferred to express his interest by giving me a handsome present. One of my seniors, however, a dear fatherly old man, when I inadvertently told him that I was going on leave to get married, looked round to see that no one else was in earshot and then whispered to me in a kindly inquisitive way; "But do your people know?" He no doubt wished to save me from a rash decision in view of what he knew of my poverty. But looking back over the long years of happiness my wife and I had together, if I had my time over again I would marry even earlier than I did.

We lived severely within our income. We entertained many friends. We never went without at least a fortnight's holiday by the sea every year, and if they were not "the happiest days of my life" it is because they have nearly all been happy. It may be difficult for young people to believe that it was possible to live quite well on the small incomes prevalent before the First World War, and they may consider that my wife and I were particularly fortunate or exceptional, but I can recall a week's holiday in Belgium with a cousin of mine in 1902 or 1903 when the whole cost – including steamer tickets from London to Ostend, a railway ticket that took us to Bruges, Brussels, the Ardennes, Antwerp and back to Ostend, complete *pension* terms, the purchase of fifty cigars, some scent, and a picture that still hangs on my walls – was £3.

My son was born in January 1910, and my daughter in May 1914. With the outbreak of war in the August of that year my life, like millions of others was disrupted, my philosophy and ideas severely challenged, and I was thrown into the experience of soldiering, which took me away from the Museum from November 1915 until July 1919.

When I was demobilized I returned immediately to my former work without even a day's holiday. This was a mistake – the change was too abrupt, and for some time I was unable to adjust myself to the possibility of a dull career, feeling disturbed, disgruntled and uncertain as to what I could do otherwise, and I tried to find some satisfaction in personal and social interests outside my official work.

Before the war I had retained my interest in the Music Department in the vague hope that eventually I should be promoted to the Assistant grade and succeed Barclay Squire, but the eventuality seemed so uncertain that I was anything but happy. To my surprise, however, the unexpected happened, and I succeeded Squire in 1920, as mentioned above.

HANDEL COLLECTIONS
IN THE BRITISH MUSEUM –
THE CUMMINGS COLLECTION

BEFORE DEALING with the later twenty-four years of my official career it is necessary to say something about the Handel Collections in the Museum, then available to the public.

The General Catalogue of Music originally included all the Handel items up to date. But in 1912 the Trustees issued the *Catalogue of Printed Music published between 1487 and 1800 now in the British Museum*. By W. Barclay Squire. Printed by order of the Trustees, 1912, 8vo, 2 vols.

This most valuable work included of course the editions of Handel within the period. At that time the modern revival of interest in the composer, or indeed of musical bibliography generally had not commenced. This is evidenced by the fact that although the catalogue was available to the public at the modest price of three guineas the two volumes, including the copies given away to major libraries and institutions and those sold, only 300 or so of the small edition of 500 copies were disposed of by the outbreak of the 1939–45 War. During that period, under the stress of paper shortages the unsold copies of Squire's *Catalogue* together with a number of other very valuable Museum publications were pulped – a sorry and much to be regretted policy. Copies of Squire's work are offered to-day at £40 or more, and many Handelians would like to obtain one.

The *Catalogue* was an extraordinary work for one man to carry out in so short a time. It would be more useful to the musical scholar if it had included more bibliographical details and descriptions of the works, but in those days the significance of descriptive cataloguing was not appreciated – and if it had been, the work would not have been completed so quickly unless more funds and staff had been available. As it stands it is a tribute to a great public servant, and a foundation upon which much subsequent musical research has been carried out.

One thing that Squire did with amazing accuracy was to supply the dates to the works listed, although in many cases more exact dates have now been discovered. This is apparent more particularly in the case of the Handel items on which so much modern research has been done. Therefore, in consulting the *Catalogue* this should be borne in mind.

In 1940 the Trustees of the British Museum issued the Second Supplement to Squire's *Catalogue*, which I had prepared, but since then the department has acquired a great deal of early printed music which is catalogued in the volumes of *Accessions* and added to the catalogue, *Old Music 1487–1800*.

Before the publication of Squire's *Catalogue of Printed Music*, a *Catalogue of Manuscript Music in the British Museum*, by Augustus Hughes-Hughes had been published in three volumes, 1906, 1908 and 1909. This did for the manuscript music what Squire did for the printed music, but it was carried out in the much more detailed and explanatory way that is essential in dealing with manuscripts. It includes a great deal of Handel material, and the descriptions and datings by Hughes-Hughes are generally exact and scholarly.

I have heard criticisms of it from time to time, but using it as I have over the years I am more than ever grateful for the work and to the quiet, kindly and helpful editor who I knew very well. This catalogue, like Squire's, was offered to the public at a modest price: Vol. I, £1 1s; Vol. II, £1 15s; Vol. III, £1 1s; and largely remained unsold. Copies of Vols. II and III, I believe, can still be obtained at the Museum.

Subsequent additions to the manuscript music, including the famous Granville collection, have not been catalogued in a separate work but only in the various volumes of *Additional Manuscripts* issued from time to time by the department, which may one day issue details of the musical items in a supplement to the Hughes-Hughes volumes.

The Granville manuscripts of fine copies of Handel's works, originally the property of Bernard Granville (1709–75), a friend of Handel's, came on the market at Sotheby's in March 1912 and were acquired by the Museum in 1915. The sale catalogue contains interesting details of the collection, and R. A. Streatfeild contributed a very full description of the manuscripts to *The Musical Antiquary*, July 1911, pp. 208–24.

In addition to the works included in these catalogues, the Museum has an enormous collection of Handel editions after 1800, and a vast amount of Handelian literature. Of special importance to Handelians is the King's Music Library with its superb collection of holograph manuscripts and copies of the composer's works, and early printed editions – referred to later. No extensive study of Handel can be undertaken without resort to the British Museum collections.

Although not a Museum publication, Barclay Squire prepared the *Catalogue of Printed Music in the Library of the Royal College of Music*, which was published in 1909, and contains many Handel items. He also made, with assistance, a typescript catalogue of the musical manuscripts in the College, including many Handel works.

Squire had a special interest in, and great knowledge of, early and Elizabethan music, and he therefore paid particular attention to the purchasing of editions of the madrigals, motets and other examples of that period. Through his foresight, limited as he was in official funds, he made the Museum collection almost complete as far as English composers were concerned, and obtained many early Italian and other foreign works.

He showed no particular interest in the field of Handelian research, although he contributed some articles on the composer's work to various journals. He held the opinion, pretty common at that time, that there was little to be known about Handel and his work additional to what Chrysander, Schœlcher, Rockstro and others had published. In fact, when later on I took up my research work, he told me that there was little chance of finding out

anything fresh about the composer. His knowledge of the bibliographical details of Handel's early editions was, like that of most
musicologists of his day, very limited. Had he been more acquainted with and interested in this subject the Museum to-day
would include many more valuable early manuscripts and editions
of Handel than it does; but this is not to discredit his valuable
services to the department, or to criticize his expenditure of
the very small official sums he had at his disposal.

Fortunately for future Handelians there was in the Department
of Printed Books a keen and very competent musical scholar who
made a special study of the composer – R. A. Streatfeild. His
book, *Handel*, published in October 1909 by Methuen & Co., is
still one of the best works on the subject – full of new matter
and discerning technical knowledge, beautifully written and
factually reliable. It did much for the renaissance and better understanding of the composer and his work, and in its way has never
been surpassed.

Writing in the preface of his work Streatfeild said:

> "It is the inner meaning of Handel's music, and its power of search-
> ing the profoundest recesses of the soul, that in the following
> pages I have endeavoured, so far as I am able, to elucidate. Its
> merely technical qualities have already been discussed enough
> and to spare. Books on Handel written by musicians already
> abound, but musicians as a rule take more interest in the means
> by which an end is attained than in the end itself. They tell us a
> great deal about the methods by which a composer expresses
> himself, but very little about what he actually has to express. I
> have tried, how feebly and with what little success no one knows
> better than myself, to find the man Handel in his music, to trace
> his character, his view of life, his thoughts, feelings and aspira-
> tions as they are set forth in his works."

No enthusiastic student of Handel can afford to be ignorant of
this informative and inspiring biography of the composer. Had
Streatfeild not unexpectedly died before Squire's retirement, I
think he would have succeeded him as Assistant in charge of the
Music Department, and my future would have been very different from what it was.

Of the private collections of music in my early days, that of W. Hayman Cummings, Principal of the Guildhall School of Music was the most famous. He bought widely and wisely, every kind and class of early and contemporary music, musical literature and miscellaneous material, including a great many of the early editions and manuscripts of Handel, and some most interesting relics of the composer. These included the copy of the Will and codicils (duplicates of those in the Probate Registry, Somerset House) now in the possession of Gerald Coke, of Bentley, Hants; *An Inventory of the Household Goods of George Frederick Handel, Esq. deceased* (now in the British Museum); an autograph letter; and *Unique Printed Documents relating to the lives of Handel and his Family* (also in the British Museum), etc.

The Cummings Collection was sold at Sotheby's over the six days, May 17–24, 1917 and fetched in all £6,488 4s 6d, but at present day prices worth very much more. The British Museum obtained a number of items at the sale, the most interesting being the three first issues of Handel's *Suites de Pieces pour le Clavecin*. The Will fetched £210. A priced copy of the catalogue, with purchasers' names, can be seen in the Museum (MR. Ref. 3c) and I have a copy in my possession.

The Aylesford, Balfour (Julian Marshall), Flower, Arkwright Fitzwilliam, Coke, Hall and other collections are dealt with later on.

THE KING'S MUSIC LIBRARY –
PERCY ROBINSON – J. C. SMITH
FATHER AND SON

WHEN I SUCCEEDED SQUIRE in 1920, although I had hoped and worked as hard as I could for this to happen there were reasons why it might not. I knew that I did not have the scholarship and background of Squire, although there was little work in the department with which I was not familiar. At the time, I learnt that there were certain members of the staff who, although not employed in the Music Section, were being backed by some in authority as likely recipients of the appointment, and the position itself appealed to some musical scholars outside the Museum as a nice harbour in which to take refuge from their professional uncertainties. Fortunately for me, although he gave me very little information about what was happening, Squire strongly endorsed my successorship. He retained a connection with the Department as he undertook to catalogue "The King's Music Library" which, largely through his influence had been deposited in the Museum on permanent loan by His Majesty King George V in 1911, and in 1957 was given to the Nation by Her Majesty Queen Elizabeth II.

Apart from many valuable miscellaneous manuscripts and much printed music the royal collection includes holograph and contemporary copies of the great majority of Handel's works. Squire's detailed catalogue of the manuscripts, in view of the absence of comprehensive research on the manuscripts themselves (other than that done by Chrysander for his edition) is essential for Handelian students. Squire had help on many of the cataloguing problems that arose from Percy Robinson, author of *Handel and his Orbit* (1908) – a fine scholar who worked quietly and effectively, hardly noticed outside his own family circle. His book, and the few articles he wrote are real contributions to the study of the composer, his works, and some of his contemporaries. I only knew him as a kindly correspondent. He died in 1947, but in 1942 had sent me his copy of *Händel und Shakespeare*, by G. G. Gervinus, for my collection.

Squire, at the time of his death in 1926 had completed the cataloguing of the Handel manuscripts and most of the printed music in the King's Collection. Hilda Andrews subsequently catalogued the miscellaneous manuscripts, and the catalogue of the whole collection was issued by the Trustees of the British Museum in three volumes, 1927–29.

Percy Robinson's invaluable articles are:

> Handel up to 1720: a new chronology. (*Music and Letters*, January, 1939, pp. 55–63.)
> Handel's Early Life and Mainwaring. (*Musical Times*, September, 1925, pp. 814–16, 820.)
> Handel's Journeys. (*Musical Antiquary*, July, 1910, pp. 193–202.)
> Was Handel a Plagiarist? (*Musical Times*, August, 1939, pp. 573–77.)

In 1912, soon after the depositing of the King's Music in the Museum, a small exhibition of some of the Handel autograph manuscripts was arranged in the public gallery (King's Library) of the Department of Printed Books, and for this Streatfeild published an interesting pamphlet, based on an article in *The Times* – "Handel Autographs at the British Museum".

For the first twenty years or more of my time at the Museum the show cases in the King's Library continued to exhibit the same early printed books and music, etc., with a very occasional special exhibition of other things. In recent years much more use has been made of opportunities to display material on special subjects, or in connection with particular literary or historical events.

It is of great satisfaction to Handelians that the composer, as I have pointed out elsewhere, had an orderly mind and a shrewd sense of the wisdom of having his manuscripts carefully preserved. There is evidence of this from his Hamburg days and during his subsequent travels in Italy. J. C. Smith (Schmidt) the elder came to London, it is said, as Handel's Secretary and Treasurer in 1716 and by 1720 had established himself in the music publishing business. Handel bequeathed to him by his Will of June 1, 1750 his "Musick Books" – assumed to mean all the music in his possession. Smith senior in his turn bequeathed these to his son J. C. Smith, junior, by his Will of December 16, 1762.

Until Smith senior's Will was traced at Somerset House through the zeal and research of Dr. James S. Hall, it was not known that Smith's death was some time in January 1763 (the Will being proved January 10) and it was assumed by Squire and others that Handel's music passed directly to J. C. Smith, junior. He did ultimately acquire the manuscripts (autographs and some copies) which he presented to George III in gratitude for a pension granted to him in 1774 or a little earlier. These manuscripts now form part of the King's Music Library, British Museum, and the catalogue of them by Squire has an important and informative introduction. Another fine collection of manuscript scores (contemporary copies with autograph additions) came presumably from the original bequest of Handel to J. C. Smith senior, then by will to his son, who left them to Lady Rivers, his stepdaughter, who presumably gave them to her son Sir Henry Rivers. Thomas Kerslake, a Bristol bookseller acquired them, from whom they were bought by Victor Schœlcher who sold them to Chrysander. Finally they were purchased through a public fund for the State and University Library of Hamburg, where they still remain.

Johann Christoph Schmidt, known to English Handelians as John Christopher Smith, was associated with Handel in London for some 40 years at least as his amanuensis and secretary. The date of his arrival here from Germany is uncertain – somewhere between 1716 and 1719. Until a few years ago little else was known about him except that his name appeared in the imprints of various Handelian publications by John Cluer and Richard Meares and that he had a son of the same name, John Christopher Smith, about whom we know a good deal. It was customary until recently to describe most of the early copies of Handel's works as Smith copies. The composer bequeathed by Will, June 1, 1750: "to Mr Christopher Smith my large Harpsicord, my little House Organ, my Musick Books, and five hundred Pounds sterl:" and by codicil, August 6, 1756 a legacy of an additional "fifteen hundred pounds".

It is not necessary here to go over what we now know of the lives of the Smiths, father and son, as recorded in the works listed below which correct some misstatements and add considerably to our knowledge of these two important people in Handel's life and work. Unfortunately we have no intimate letters, documents or reports of the personal associations of the composer and Smith senior. What a lot the old man could have told us about his master and friend, if he had only written a few letters or left behind some reminiscences. As we now know the music went to Smith the elder, who bequeathed to his son "All my Musick Books and Peices of Musick whether Manuscript or otherwise which were left to me by the last Will & Testament of my Friend George Frederick Handel deceased and also all my other Musick & Books of Musick both in print & manuscript and all my Instruments of Musick".

As mentioned above most of the manuscripts are now in the King's Music Library, British Museum, and others ultimately found a resting place in the State and University Library, Hamburg, with a few scattered about here and there.

The intricate problems of identifying manuscripts actually written by Smith senior were not undertaken seriously until Professor Larsen made a special study of the subject and published his findings in his monumental *Handel's Messiah. Origins – Composition – Sources* (Adam & Charles Black, London, 1957). Not only does Professor Larsen give facsimiles of the genuine Smith hands, but at great length and in detail examines and gives facsimiles of many other manuscripts by other copyists which have been confused with or described as Smith copies. Other scholars

3

have dealt with individual manuscripts, and Dr. James S. Hall has made a first survey of the manuscripts in the collection of Sir Newman Flower, and related them to Professor Larsen's examples.

It would be interesting to know what system of working existed between Handel and Smith, the latter having presumably employed other copyists for some of the manuscripts, and what was the rate and method of payment. Was the main source of Smith's income as Handel's copyist, other than what he received from his brief association with music publishing and Handel's generous bequests?

The following is a list of the principal articles that give us information about the Smiths outside the usual biographies of Handel or the musical dictionaries:

> More Handeliana. William C. Smith. (*Music and Letters*, January 1953, pp. 11–15.) This includes a transcript of the Will of J. C. Smith the younger.
>
> John Christopher Smith. Handel's Friend and Secretary. By James S. Hall. (*Musical Times*, March, 1955, pp. 132–34.) This contains a transcript of the Will of J. C. Smith the elder and much about the Smiths.
>
> Neue Daten zu Johann Christoph Schmidt, von Konrad Sasse. (*Händel-Jahrbuch* . . . 3. (IX.) Jahrgang 1957. Deutscher Verlag für Musik, Leipzig, pp. 115–25.) This is a learned enquiry into Smith's German origins and relations.
>
> John Christopher Smith: his residence in London. By James S. Hall. (*Händel-Jahrbuch* . . . 3. (IX.) Jahrgang 1957. Deutscher Verlag für Musik, Leipzig, pp. 133–37.) A detailed report on the premises and addresses in Soho, London, occupied by Smith the elder from time to time. On this subject and many other details of the Smith circle and his descendants there is much material in the hands of Dr. Hall still unpublished.
>
> *Anecdotes of George Frederick Handel and John Christopher Smith.* London, 1799. Wrongly attributed to William Coxe, it is the foundation work on Smith the younger, and contains an engraving of Smith's portrait by Zoffany, now in the possession of Gerald Coke.
>
> John Christopher Smith as a dramatic composer. By Andrew D. McCredie. (*Music and Letters*, January, 1964, pp. 22–38.)

4

THE MUSIC DEPARTMENT
BRITISH MUSEUM 1920-44

TO BE IN CHARGE of the Music Department was attractive to me for a number of reasons. First of all, I could not help feeling proud that my indisciplined efforts to acquire the necessary knowledge and my past record did not put me out of the running. Secondly, I knew that if I were interfered with as little by my Principals as Squire had been by his, it would accord very well with my personal temperament and wishes. I could always work enthusiastically if left alone, and Squire had always given me plenty of scope for doing whatever I thought necessary in the department. Thirdly, it had been understood for some years that when opportunity afforded, the Music Department would be moved to the fine, pleasant rooms which it occupies to-day – in what was then the new North Wing of the Museum. If this were to take place I should escape from the rather dull room of the general library in which I had spent so many years, and which had become all too small to accommodate the music collection, much of which was badly housed in other parts of the library. Fourthly, if we did move to the proposed new quarters I could count on comparative peace and quiet in which to carry out my duties.

Well, so it happened. We moved into the new wing in 1922, to which the King's Music Library had already been transferred earlier – a special room having been set apart for the purpose. With the assistance of Charles Humphries, a colleague who had been with me since September, 1907, I was able to arrange for the removal of the collection, and its lay-out in its new quarters.

It was a joy to live in a room with north, south and west windows, ample table space and plenty of shelf room to allow for expansion (as we considered then) for the next fifty years at least. To be on the safe side, we also laid claim to some spare space in the basement, which gave us in all some two miles of shelving.

The ordinary work of cataloguing, etc. went on under my control, in the main much as formerly, with minor modifications in method and procedure. I considered in what essential ways the system could be modified to advantage, and concluded that our long established practices, well understood by the staff and readers, needed no serious alteration; and I think it can be generally accepted that unless you can very quickly completely reorganize and re-catalogue a large library it is rather open to question whether it is worth while disturbing it for many years, or introducing new methods drastically in conflict with old ones.

There was, however, one major problem that I had always felt needed attention, and which I was determined to deal with if I ever became Assistant in charge of the Music. This was the vast accumulation and steadily growing mass of uncatalogued sheet-music of various kinds. When Squire found himself being swamped by masses of music-hall songs, dance music, and other unimportant items, he obtained authority, or at least I assumed he did, to keep these works out of the printed catalogues of accessions. Unfortunately, when he had separated such works from those that had to be catalogued, he didn't bother much as to what happened to them, other than to hand them over to an elderly official in a minor position, whose job it was to do them up in parcels and place them anywhere, as long as they could be found when wanted. Fortunately for Squire and the Department this official, a poorly paid, unpensioned member of the bindery staff, named Lister, was a man with an orderly mind and a very good memory. To the best of his ability he dealt with the problem by making up parcels of music in their various categories and series, and with some regard to dates of publication and alphabetical order. No one but Lister knew what his system was, and if *he* could not find a work that was asked for, it was assumed that it had never been received. When I took over, the number and kinds of parcels were alarming and as, owing to the revival of old music-hall and popular songs for use in films, plays and on the radio, there was an increasing demand for such items, it was becoming imperative that we should have some system under which, if a reader, owner of the copyright, or other applicant gave us the information that would be necessary to find a required work not in the catalogue, it ought to be possible to find such a work, if it existed among the uncatalogued music.

Humphries and I devised such a scheme – simple and fairly fool-proof – which entailed breaking up all the heterogeneous parcels, and re-sorting the whole of the uncatalogued music into the two main divisions – vocal and instrumental – subdivided into periods of ten years, and placed alphabetically under the composers' names or titles. This system worked admirably, and in course of time lent itself to a simple slip indexing under titles or composers. The major part of this work fell upon Humphries and occupied him for some years.

It is not necessary to record here all the attempts we made to add to the accessibility or usefulness of the music collection. But as time went on, many more demands were made upon us by the public than in Squire's day, and we had to find answers to new problems as these arose. One necessary improvement we were able to undertake was the preparation for use in the Reading Room and in the Department, of a Catalogue of National Music. Another was a subject slip-index of the music up to the end of the eighteenth century. But there were dozens of jobs that should have been done had we had the necessary staff and more money to spend.

It was always regrettable to me that this fine collection did not have a larger staff to deal with it more effectively, and more spent on its development. It suffered as the rest of the Department of Printed Books did in those days, from lack of imagination on the part of some of those in authority as to what should be done, from failure to demand larger sums from the public funds, and from the long standing practice of the Treasury in refusing most requests for additional staff or money. It is essential for public servants to feel that they have an inflexible duty to see that every pound spent on their authority is wisely spent within the framework of their particular service; but it is ludicrous that even the appointment of a temporary clerk, or the granting of a special increment of £10 have to be subjects of long correspondence between the head of a department and the Treasury, whilst every now and again permission can be obtained to pay out considerable lump sums for particular objects, the financial or cultural value of which is often doubtful.

During the years that I was in charge of the music, there was a special call for national economy as the result of the 1914—18 War, and the more stringent circumstances of the later conflict. Consequently, it was no use constantly bombarding the various Keepers of Printed Books for more staff or money. If Squire or I had had the latter, many valuable accessions of old music and modern foreign works could have been made at comparatively trifling cost. As it was, I spent the little I was allowed, and shut my eyes to the many treasures I should have liked the department to acquire, some of which I was able to purchase for myself.

Recognizing that there was a limited amount of work that the department could do I tried to keep up to date all the cataloguing and other jobs in hand rather than attempt a number of fresh tasks that I could not possibly continue to carry on with my small staff. Fortunately, my successor has not been faced with the same problems so acutely. His staff has been considerably increased. He has had a few years of almost (as it seems to me) lavish expenditure, and the support of a Principal Keeper of Printed Books, Dr. C. B. Oldman, C.B., a distinguished musicologist, and his successor R. A. Wilson, C.B., who have both been more concerned officially in the development of the Music Department than some of their predecessors were.

Two very regrettable illustrations can be given of useful schemes in the department that stopped because it was impossible under the then existing circumstances to continue them. One was a Catalogue of Authors of words set to music in any form – songs, cantatas, operas, etc. This was maintained up to some time in the latter quarter of the nineteenth century. Squire did not keep it up, no doubt because he had no staff to continue it. It was a most useful source of reference, and listed many writers of words otherwise unknown, and literary works that only appeared in published music. To my horror, I found when I came back to the Museum after the 1914—18 War, that the long existing volumes of this special catalogue had been destroyed for space reasons, or may-be as salvage – I never dared ask. It would have been considered an impertinence.

The other example of work that should have been continued is a slip catalogue of all the libretti in the Museum, with an index of authors. This was compiled largely by Squire up to about 1918, and entailed the gigantic task of reading through all the existing volumes of the General Catalogue in order to pick out the libretti. It would have been comparatively easy for somebody detailed for the purpose to note and catalogue all the libretti subsequently acquired by the Museum and appearing in the accession parts. But again, nobody troubled to see that this was done.

Some of the many supplementary jobs I should have liked to have undertaken were catalogues, or lists, of the various publishers, engravers and printers of music; details of illustrations and illustrators; particulars of sale catalogues, and indexes of such of these as are of sufficient importance; indexes of song-books and other collections; and lists of subscribers to early works. Some of these tasks are, I understand, already in hand, and they are only indications of the fact that librarians' work is never complete.

In my young days at the Museum the whole place, particularly the Department of Printed Books, was "dusted" by a group of male cleaners under the command of an old ex-soldier – one Francis; and a real Fred Karno's troupe they were! They moved around at a snail's pace; they had a marvellous technique for doing nothing very busily, and their conversation was as colourful, as entertaining and as comic as that recorded of working-men in the pages of some of our greatest observers of human nature in the rough. Their method of dusting was ludicrous – damp cloths, and perhaps a year or two's gap in between their operations on any particular part of the library. At one time, an attempt was made to deal with the dust more effectively by using a large vacuum cleaner, which operated outside the building, with a heavy suction pipe leading to the particular shelves. This was treated like the Luddites treated the machines a hundred and fifty years or so ago, except that the cleaners did not smash the vacuum cleaner – but only made it unworkable. So they came back with their dusters and their own method of carrying on, which entailed dirt and filth generally on the great majority of books, other than those in cases or those recently dusted. When I moved into my nice clean rooms in the new wing I decided I was going to do something about having them kept clean, and I managed to succeed in this fairly well. I arranged (how, I don't remember) to have a permanent male "duster", who cleaned the floors, tables and desks every day as far as possible, and I saw to it that a small band of others came up regularly and worked over the music on the shelves. I thought that I could get the men to use small vacuum cleaners, two or three of which I understood existed in the Museum, and which could easily be run from the electric light points. But no, I was wrong. They saw to it; bulbs were always being broken and the machines constantly out of order – so I let them have their way with the damp cloths.

Looking back now, I can see that I was frequently guilty of doing things and making decisions, when I should have referred matters to the Keeper; but as I knew that I should probably get no for an answer to any suggested proposals of mine to some of my superiors, I did the better thing – asked no questions and got, as I thought, the right results. Stowed away as my department was, a long way from the Keeper's room, I lived a life of comfortable detachment from the Library as a whole; but I gathered from more than one incident, that I was looked upon quite favourably as far as the running of the department was concerned, but as a not altogether easy person to persuade. I wish now that I had been much bolder and more self-opinionated, and had taken more drastic action about certain things, without consulting anybody. I remember one chief, who considered that I was always wanting privileges for the work and maintenance of the Music Section, telling me: "You must be reasonable!". Soon afterwards he brought some distinguished librarian from overseas round the department, and as he introduced me, said to the visitor: "This is the most satisfactory section of the Library". Another chief on one occasion, when he was splendidly defending me against some charge of having transgressed official etiquette, said to his superior: "And what's more, Smith is one of the people who have never asked for anything!" – a back-handed compliment in a way.

I could never compete with Squire in scholarship and knowledge, neither could I exceed the speed with which he did the amazing amount of his work. When I joined him, I remember he said that the chief thing was to have a good memory. That, I considered, was not lacking in me, and I found as the years went by that although other things were essential – knowledge of the history and practice of music; general education and wide reading – memory was, after all, vital for the quick and effective performance of one's duties.

I knew that Squire had specialized in Elizabethan and pre-Elizabethan music, and that it was largely due to him that the collection was so rich in such items, so I determined to concentrate my personal private study on the eighteenth century, a period that had always interested me socially and historically, and about which I had read a good deal. This partly explains my subsequent interest in, and contributions to, the study of Handel and his contemporaries. I must point out here, what is known to many students of the period, that the eighteenth century is largely an undocumented time in English musical history. There are a considerable number of composers and performers whose lives and works await satisfactory studies, biographies and critical appraisements. There are hundreds of songs, keyboard and other pieces worth editing and publishing, while the bibliography of the period is still in its infancy. I have frequently pointed this out to students and others who have been considering what field of study they should interest themselves in, and I have often regretted that I did not undertake more serious research when I first entered the Museum. Whatever has been done on any subject, further knowledge can often be obtained by working over the ground covered by others.

One of the pleasant features of my work was attending to the miscellaneous correspondence which came from scholars and students in all parts of the world asking for help and advice on musical questions. Most of the correspondents opened up subjects that entailed some research on my part, and consequently I was always widening my knowledge and, what was more important, becoming better acquainted with the treasures under my care. In those days we had no typists, and unless one took the trouble to make copies of letters by hand there was no record kept of the answers given. By this official correspondence I made many pleasing contacts and some firm friends.

The British Museum has always been the Mecca to which visitors of all kinds and of every country come for one purpose or another, and the Music Department has its steady stream of visitors, all of whom are welcome if they have a reasonable purpose and ordinary manners. I mention this latter because occasionally somebody or other with an exaggerated sense of his own importance transgresses the rules of courtesy and decency, and makes himself objectionable. On such occasions my hot temper sometimes came to boiling point and I am afraid I did not present the visitor with the calm of official behaviour.

One reader from the Reading Room, having been told that some music he wanted was being bound, was brought to me to know whether we could get the work up from the Binder's Shop – a procedure which was sometimes adopted in such cases. I explained that unfortunately the Binder's Shop was shut, as it was the workers' dinner-time. This made the reader furious; he raged and stormed, saying that we did nothing but eat and sleep. My answer was to throw his application ticket on to the floor, point to the door and tell him to go out the way he came in. He reported this to the Keeper, a very wise and balanced chief, who sent for me and told me of the complaint, and asked me what had happened. I told him, and added that I should feel like doing the same to any other reader who was similarly rude to me and made such unjustified accusations about the Department. The Keeper smiled, and admitted that there were some very troublesome readers.

As I have said elsewhere, in my early days I used to wonder how the distinguished scholars I met fitted in to my small world, but as I got to know them more intimately I found behind most of them a man who was something other than a great scholar or learned research worker – and this human element often came out in their side interests, habits and associations. One who was looked upon as a great authority in a specialized field, once told me in all sincerity that Dan Leno and Albert Chevalier were two of the greatest men of his day. It was not unusual to find this same delightful Head of a department shooting at the pigeons with a peashooter out of his window because they were taking the bread he had put out for the sparrows, and following up his good shots with: "Got you, you ——!"

One of the most interesting and delightful people I met at the Museum was Professor Dayton C. Miller, a great American scientist who, as a sideline to his work as a physicist had interested himself in "The Science of Sound", on which he wrote an *Anecdotal History*. He made a special study of the flute, published a bibliography on the subject, and had a very large collection of the instruments, including one which formerly belonged to Frederick the Great. Professor Miller visited the Museum each year from 1926 onwards for a few years. He gave me copies of his books and a collection of photographs of all the flutes and allied instruments in his possession, which are now in the Library of Congress, Washington. What impressed me very much about Professor Miller was not only his courtesy and kindness but the absence of any emphasis on the importance of himself or his work, great scientist as he was.

I met, of course, many famous musicians and others in my official capacity – Toscanini, Cortot, Elgar, Alfred Einstein, Peter Warlock, Henry Wood, just to name a few; but it is impossible to deal here in detail with this side of my work, as over the years the number of visitors to the Music Department was considerable.

When the 1939–45 War broke out the Museum was faced with

an anticipated problem – what to do to safeguard its treasures against aerial attack. The general plans are outside the scope of this story; suffice it to say here that some departments were removed entirely elsewhere; but as it was necessary for various reasons to keep the Library and Reading Rooms open, selections were made of certain items to be removed, and the remainder had to run the risk of being destroyed. Of the music, I selected for removal the whole of the Handel manuscripts, all the early printed and Elizabethan music, and some other special works, while Humphries and I remained to carry on our duties at Bloomsbury as best we could. Fortunately, the Music Department escaped damage except for a broken window or two; but we often had to rush to safer quarters on the ground floor when the raiders were about.

In some of the empty steel cased shelves I housed my own collection (without official permission, I am afraid), as I considered the six-feet-thick walls of the British Museum could stand up to things better than my small suburban house, which, however, survived although damaged, but not seriously.

We were thoroughly instructed in what to do when an "alert" was given, as the authorities had made quite long-prepared and effective local plans for dealing with emergencies, including the provision of what were considered safe and well conditioned air-raid shelters in the basement, to which we were directed to go. The first time we had an "alert", down we all went, taking up our respective places. We sat about, waiting, thinking, talking, wondering what we should do next. After perhaps an hour or more of this official inactivity the Keeper of Printed Books, who was in the shelter to which I had to go, left us. Twenty minutes or so later he returned with a cold meat pie and other food which he had been able to find in his wife's pantry at the official house where he lived. We divided this food up rather like the loaves and fishes in the parable, solemnly ate our quota, and then went on waiting until the "all-clear" went, when we trooped back to our work. That was the end of a well intentioned safety scheme. Most of us never went down to the air-raid shelters again during office hours; finding, like the average Londoner, that one's job had to go on in spite of Hitler, and it was that spirit in the end which turned Hitler's own shelter into the place where the maniac could face things no longer.

5

THE NEWMAN FLOWER COLLECTION –
THE AYLESFORD MANUSCRIPTS

IT WAS A FORTUNATE DAY for me when I first met Newman,
afterwards Sir Newman Flower. In October, 1920, he wrote to
Barclay Squire, who had then retired, for advice about what he
considered was a first edition of the score of Handel's *Messiah*, and
some other early editions. The Keeper of that day, rather given to
laconic brevity in dealing with me, minuted on the letter:
"Please be prepared to see this man if he brings his books"; and
so I did, thus beginning an acquaintanceship that rapidly developed
into a friendship that lasted until Flower's death, with increasing
pleasure to both of us. Flower came up by appointment and I gave
him what information I could about the score. He told me that
he was intending to form a Handel collection and write a biography of the composer, and asked me if I would undertake
certain work for him in this connection. I readily agreed, and
made this my chief unofficial occupation for a number of years.
I was also associated with him in the preparation of his biographies
of Schubert and Sullivan; but these were only passing fancies to
me, compared with my growing interest in Handel.

Among the half dozen or so famous public or private collections of Handel's works and Handeliana, Newman Flower's
is exceptional in one important respect. It includes most of
the one time famous Aylesford manuscripts of the scores and
parts, vocal and instrumental, of the operas, oratorios and many
other works. These are all fine copies specially made for Charles
Jennens, the compiler of *Messiah*, and a friend of Handel's. They
can in many cases be accepted as the authentic versions – even

when they differ from the autographs. The British Museum and other libraries and collectors have autograph scores and copies, but instrumental and vocal manuscript parts are of the utmost rarity outside Flower's collection, and no definitive and scholarly modern edition can be satisfactorily prepared without recourse to these manuscripts. Why similar parts do not exist in the British Museum and elsewhere is probably explained by the fact that Handel, who was most careful (as I have said) to see that his scores were safely preserved while on his early travels and eventually in his permanent home in Brook Street, London, kept the instrumental and vocal parts elsewhere – presumably at the King's Theatre and Covent Garden. As we know, both these theatres were burnt down later and their contents destroyed.

The Aylesford family started disposing of their miscellaneous music as early as August 25, 1873 (BM.S.CP.157(14)), but the major sale of Handel's manuscripts and music was in May 1918. Much of this went ultimately, as described above, to Newman Flower, who also acquired items from various other sources. The Library of Congress in Washington D.C. has some manuscripts from the 1918 sale, and Barclay Squire bought a few, which he presented to the King's Music Library. It is true that the sale was in the dark war days of the Spring of 1918, but even bearing that in mind it is surprising that Squire did not buy the whole collection for the Museum for the few pounds that it fetched. A number of sample items from the priced sale catalogue will suffice:

> Rodelinda, Radamisto, Poro and Partenope. MS. Scores. 5/–
> Amadis, MS. Score, red morocco, tooled edges; and MS. Scores of Tamerlane, Teseo, Silla, Semele, Berenice and Siroe; also Cembalo and Six Parts of Silla, Amadis and Radamisto. 10/–
> Tamerlane, MS. Score; and Six Part Books (Tamerlane and Rodelinda). 3/–
> Rinaldo MS. Score and Cembalo and eight Parts of Rinaldo, Pastor Fido and Teseo; MS. Scores of Agrippino and Roderigo, with Cembalo and Six Parts; Scipio, MS. Score, Cembalo and Six Parts. 9/–

These prices are typical of the whole sale. The Aylesford family must have been very sick at the result, the dealers and other purchasers very pleased, and the British Museum was very unfortunate.

Newman Flower's *George Frideric Handel* was published by Cassell & Co. in 1923, and achieved a large circulation. It did much to bring the life and personality of the composer before the reading public. It did not pretend to be a technical study of Handel's works, but a readable biography; and as such it is full of colour and interest, with many illustrations. To quote from Flower's Preface:

> "No attempt has been made in this volume to survey the works of Handel in any technical sense, nor to deal with his music in any technical form ... I have endeavoured rather, to outline Handel the Man – the striking personality who never admitted defeat, but rose superior to whatever powers a surfeit of enemies could and did exert. In order to convey, however poorly, this Handel, I have attempted to sketch a background of the times in which he lived, and the people with whom he had to deal."

My special contribution to the book was the "Bibliography", the most comprehensive that had appeared up to that time. It was work in the preparation of this that revealed to me the need for much more research into the study of Handel, his work and his times. The book has gone through several subsequent editions and translations, and has certainly played a great part in the renaissance of Handel that has taken place in the last forty years or so.

Flower's collection includes, besides the valuable manuscripts, copies of the early printed editions; five fine large size contemporary portraits and other Handeliana – rings, miniatures, etc., prints, rare libretti and much literature, some items of which are listed below. An early and incomplete catalogue of the collection was privately issued in 1921, and Dr. James S. Hall of Walmer, Kent, has carried out a First Survey of the Aylesford manuscripts, which is only available in private typescript copies – in the collections of Flower, Hall and myself.

The Flower collection of Handel manuscripts is bound up in about 300 volumes, containing some 700 separate items, some of which deserve special mention:

Two manuscript scores of *Messiah*, one in three volumes, the second Vols. I and III only, not autograph, identified by Dr. Hall as in the hand of Prof. Larsen's S.2, S.5, respectively, with some miscellaneous parts.

Songs in *Jupiter in Argos*, bound up with "Tunes compos'd for the Playhouse" (music of *The Alchemist*), the Overture in score and eleven numbers from *Orestes* (pasticcio).

Score of the *Water Music* (movements in different order to Walsh), and fourteen parts.

Handel autographs in the collection are:

Ouverture in Flavio. Mr. Handel's own handwriting. 3 pp. The gift of Mr. John Daniel d'Luski to Samuel Felsted, Organist of St. Andrew's, 1774. (Sotheby Catalogue, June 27, 1932.)

Theodora. An Oratorio. The libretto in the Autograph of Dr. Thomas Morell with autograph note: "I intend to perform this Oratorio at the Theatre Royal in Covent Garden George Frideric Handel". (From Cummings collection, with note by him.)

Libretti:

Nero. Hamburg, 1705.

Der Beglückte Florindo. Hamburg, 1708.

La Resurettione. Roma, 1708.

Oriana. (German edition of *Amadis*.) Hamburg, 1717.

Cleofida. (German edition of *Poro*.) Hamburg, 1732.

A Description of the Machine for the Fireworks with all its Ornaments . . . in St. James's Park, Thursday, April 27, 1749, etc. London, W. Bowyer, etc., 1749.

Songs in Messiah. (No. 3. Smith Catalogue.)

The Songs in Messiah. (No. 5. Smith Catalogue.)

Many Walsh and other editions of the Operas, Oratorios, Vocal and Instrumental Works, the early ones of which are all listed in the Smith Catalogue – some 200 items.

Beethoven's Autograph Copy of Four Movements from Handel's Twelve Grand Concertos in Seven Parts. Opera 6.

Original Score of *Der Winterabend*, by Franz Schubert. Autograph.

Handel Portraits. Five large paintings: Hudson, Hogarth, Denner and two others, artists unknown.

Miniatures: Hudson, from Cummings collection. Another, small, on silk.

Gold Ring. Presented to Rev. Charles Wesley by H.M. George

III. With inscription, "George Frederick Handel Esq. Born Feb‍y 24, 1684. Died April 14, 1759." With miniature portrait of Handel, after Hudson.
Silver Medal Halle. 250th Handel birthday anniversary celebration, 1935. Presented to Sir Newman Flower.
Silver Medal. Handel Commemoration, 1784.
Bronze Medal. Handel Centenary Celebration, Crystal Palace, 1859.
C. F. Zincke. Miniature Portrait on copper, believed to be James, First Duke of Chandos.

The Collection also includes early manuscripts of instrumental and vocal works by G. M. Alberti, T. Albinoni, G. Bencini, P. P. Bencini, G. Boni, Corelli, F. Giardini, F. Kotzwara, Cardinal Pietro Ottoboni, A. Scarlatti, L. Somis, F. M. Veracini, Vivaldi and others.

One of the most important items is the unique manuscript copy of the Score and fourteen Instrumental Parts of *The Water Musick*. This work has always been a problem for editors, as there is no autograph or complete early edition of the whole work. As described in the article, "The Earliest Editions of the Water Music" (*Concerning Handel*, pp. 269–87), Walsh issued a set of Parts c. 1733, and a more complete edition for the Harpsichord, 1743. The contents of these two editions are listed in *Concerning Handel* under references A–U. (Instrumental Parts) and Nos. 1–21 (Harpsichord edition). The contents and order of the movements in Flower's copy are in these lists as follows: 1, 2, 3, A, B, C, D, E, 4, 5, 10, 11, F, G, 6, 7, 8, 9, H, I, J, K, P, Q, R, S, T, U, L, M, N, O, 14, 15, 16, 17, 18, 19, 20, 21, 12 and 13. This is a different order to that of the movements in the Fitzwilliam (Barrett Lennard) copy, in Arnold's edition and in Chrysander.

The fourteen parts in Flower's copy are: Corno Primo, Corno 2do, Violino Primo Concertino, Violino 2do Concertino, Viola, Violoncello, Basson, Contra Basso, Violino Primo Repieno, Violino 2do Repieno, Tromba Prima, Tromba 2da, Haubois Primo, Haubois 2do.

"The Famous Water Peice Compos'd by Mr. Handel", a spurious edition of *The Water Music* was published by Daniel

Wright (1733) and John Johnston (c. 1745) and has been accepted by some as adding new movements to the original work. This is not correct. It consists of 5 items only, the first from *The Water Music*; numbers 2 and 3 not identified as by Handel; numbers 4 and 5 found together as a March by Handel (BM. Add. MSS. 34126, ff. 71, 72 and elsewhere), number 5 being from Handel's *Partenope*. (See Smith. "Handel. A Descriptive Catalogue", etc. p. 257.)

The Catalogue of Schœlcher's Collection in Paris includes 56 editions, arrangements and adaptations of *The Water Music* in addition to the original issues by Walsh.

The *Illustrierte Hallische Nachrichten*, of April 11, 1936, includes an account of the visit of Frau Dr. Liebernam and Fräulein Cohauss, of the Deutsch-Englische Kulturaustauch to the home of Newman Flower, at Idehurst, Sevenoaks, with illustrations of the house and the collection, which was transferred to Tarrant Keynston House, Blandford, Dorset, where Flower died in 1964.

6

GEORGE III,
HANDEL AND MAINWARING –
PUBLICATIONS ON "MESSIAH"
1874–1928

WHEN NEWMAN FLOWER's biography of the composer was published, I felt that I could probably write a few articles on aspects of Handel and his works, not dealt with elsewhere. I had great luck with my first venture. The Museum has five copies of Mainwaring's *Memoirs of the Life of the Late George Frederic Handel*, published anonymously in 1760, and I discovered that one copy, which belongs to the Royal collection of books formerly owned by George III and acquired by the British Museum in 1823, contained many manuscript notes which on examination seemed to me to be by George III himself. Other Handelians were unaware of them, so after working over the notes very carefully, with the help of the late Edmund S. J. van der Straeten with the German used in a few cases, I wrote my first article, "George III, Handel and Mainwaring", which appeared in *The Musical Times*, September 1, 1924. I felt when it was published that it was something new in the Handelian story, and an encouragement to try again. It brought an interesting letter to the editor of *The Musical Times*, November 1, 1924, from W. H. Gratton Flood, an enthusiastic and competent musicologist, from whom I had many friendly letters afterwards.

Some of the royal comments are witty; some caustic – all of interest. One example must suffice: Referring to the use of French horns and other wind instruments in the production of *Agrippina* in Venice, the manuscript note reads:

"N.B. Forest Horns is the true appellation of that excellent instrument; the French call them Hunting Horns; and only the Land of Fools calls them French Horns. There is not a player on that or any other Wind Instrument but Bohemians, Saxons, or Hannoverians. The English are too fond of Vice and Discord to have any turn for musick".

I knew that Handel had been badly neglected with regard to the bibliographical and technical details of the early editions. There was no accurate list or thematic catalogue such as had been published for Mozart, Beethoven, Schubert, Bach and other of the great composers, but I realized that the preparation of such a catalogue would mean years of research. I therefore decided to attempt the study of one work only – the most famous and universally known of them all – *Messiah*.

My first contribution to the subject appeared in *The Musical Times*, November 1, 1925, as "The Earliest Editions of Handel's *Messiah* (New light on an old subject)". It was a happy and auspicious choice – I seem to have been investigating and writing about *Messiah* ever since. The literature on the subject is enormous. I have nearly 300 index slips of books and articles on the oratorio that I have collected. For 150 years the work was generally accepted, not only as a musical masterpiece but as an expression of the eighteenth and early nineteenth centuries' presentation of the conventional Christian story of the sacrifice of Christ and the redemption of mankind.

The earliest editions are recorded in my *Handel Catalogue*, (Cassell & Co., 1960) but Schœlcher lists in addition some forty editions up to about the middle of the nineteenth century.

The work, as is well known, was performed in all sorts of ways and places by small groups and village choirs to the master Festival choirs and orchestras of the Crystal Palace, with their thousands of voices and instruments, and the major Albert Hall and Royal Festival Hall performances of to-day. Throughout the nineteenth century, from the early days of Novello & Co., the only available vocal and instrumental scores and parts were those published by this enterprising firm; but from the beginning of this century or thereabouts there has been increasing enquiry and research as to which should be accepted as being the most authentic versions, the correct interpretation of the early manuscripts, and how the work should be performed. Of the many writers on the subject a few are mentioned here and others later on:

W. G. Cusins, Master of the Music to Queen Victoria, published in 1874 an important foundation pamphlet: *Handel's Messiah. An Examination of the Original and some of the Contemporary MSS.* (Augener & Co., London.)

James C. Culwick issued anonymously in Dublin, 1891: *Handel's Messiah. Discovery of the original word-book used at the first performance in Dublin, April 13, 1742. With some notes.*

A notable contribution was of course Chrysander's Full Score, for the German Handel Society – not completed by him on account of his death in 1901, but finished and published with a Preface by Max Seiffert in 1902.

Streatfeild in his biography of Handel (pp. 284–301) struck a new and revolutionary note in the understanding and interpretation of the oratorio which demands the attention of any serious student of the work. His main thesis is that:

> "The *Messiah* is not only a great work of art, but it is actually the first instance in the history of music of an attempt to view the mighty drama of human redemption from an artistic standpoint".

He develops his subject with great insight and effectiveness, avoiding the absurdities of some modern writers who, anxious to deny the spiritual implications of the work, pretend that it is pure humanism – as widely publicised in East Germany to-day, and by some English critics.

A successful attempt to present in handy form a "Handbook of Hints and Aids to its Public Performance", was J. Allanson Benson's *Handel's "Messiah", the Oratorio and its History* (William Reeves, London, 1923). I met the author as a reader at the Museum in the early twenties, then an elderly man, but an enthusiastic Handelian and a fine musical scholar. His was a retiring and unassuming personality, or his work would have been more widely known. He prepared a full score of *Messiah* based on his own research, but it was never published and I do not know what became of it. He was very helpful and encouraging to me. I and my wife were frequent guests at his house in Bromley, Kent, where he had a fine musical library, from which I was allowed by his widow to select any books or scores that I liked. This I did with a certain amount of hesitancy, not wishing to appear greedy. One of the scores I could have had was the 1902 Chrysander, but I felt that in selecting it I would be taking too much. By the irony of fate, years afterwards, when I wished to acquire a copy of this important edition for my collection, I enquired of a dealer as to whether he had one in stock. He said, "Yes". I agreed to purchase it at the quite expensive but not out-of-the-way price quoted – to find that it was the Benson copy which I could have had for nothing years before.

Conductors could probably learn a lot about the oratorio (tempo, interpretation, accent, etc.) from Benson's little booklet, which was followed by similar works by E. C. Bairstow, (1928); H. Watkins Shaw, (1946); Percy M. Young, (1951); R. Dalley-Scarlett, (Brisbane, 1952) and others, some of whom are referred to again in my later notes on *Messiah*.

Bairstow's *Handel's Oratorio "The Messiah"* (O.U.P. London, 1928) is especially worthy of mention here, as like Benson's booklet, it is a scholarly analysis of the oratorio, before the works on *Messiah* by Shaw, Tobin and others had appeared some twenty years later, when there was a period of intensive enquiry and research into the problems of interpretation and performance of the oratorio.

7

HANDEL CELEBRATIONS,
EXHIBITIONS, PERFORMANCES,
1935–39

A WIDENING INTEREST in Handel's works, other than *Messiah* and the one or two other popular ones, was shown in England and Germany from 1935 onwards – sparked off by celebrations for the two-hundred-and-fiftieth anniversary of the composer's birth. Leaving for later consideration the Continental performances, some of the English events were as follows:

The British Museum's contribution to the celebration was an exhibition, opened on May 11, 1935, of over sixty items of Handeliana – manuscripts, printed editions, mezzotints, engravings, drawings, medals, admission tickets, etc. I had the privilege of arranging this exhibition, but unfortunately no catalogue of it was issued. It was, however, very fully reported by Havergal Brian in *Musical Opinion*, April, 1935.

On December 23, 1934, and early in 1935, Julian Herbage was responsible for a B.B.C. performance of *Messiah*, in three parts, conducted by Adrian Boult, with the original instrumentation as far as possible – a departure from the conventional interpretations. This material was lost by enemy action and Julian Herbage edited the score again for the bi-centenary of the first performance of *Messiah* in 1942, which he conducted. His version was used for the Decca recording of the oratorio, conducted by Sir Adrian Boult. Then in February 1935, the same enthusiastic and scholarly musician, Julian Herbage, who has been over the years an inspiring force in musical education (especially with his B.B.C. weekly review with Anna Instone, *Music*

Magazine), produced a score of Handel's full-scale Ballet, *Terpsichore*, which was broadcast by the B.B.C. February 21, 1935, and repeated July 10 of that year. Herbage made the English translation and conducted the performances.

The forgotten *Jupiter in Argos*, with a new libretto entitled *Perseus and Andromeda* by Albert W. Latham, score by Julian Herbage assisted by Ralph Greaves, was broadcast by the B.B.C. October 8, 1935, and an article by Herbage on the work appeared in *The Listener*, October 2, 1935. He also edited and superintended recording sessions of *Acis and Galatea*, conducted by Sir Adrian Boult for L'Oiseau Lyre, Paris. *Acis and Galatea*; concert versions of *Rodelinda* and *Solomon* were also given by the B.B.C. in 1935.

A Handel Festival organized by the Cambridge University Musical Society was held at Cambridge from June 9–14, 1935, with a commemorative Exhibition at the Fitzwilliam Museum of Handeliana and Bach items, and performances of the Cantata *Apollo e Dafne*; the Cantata in praise of Handel, *Handel non può mia musa*; dramatic performances of *The Choice of Hercules*, and *Susanna* (produced by Camille Prior, music under the direction of Bernhard Ord and Hubert Middleton); and of other choral and orchestral music were given. (*See* also p. 103.)

An exhibition of Handel and Bach autographs was arranged in the Bodleian Library at Oxford in May 1935.

These are only some of the events that indicate a new interest in Handel – or rather, an interest in a new Handel. From then on, an increasing number of hitherto practically unknown works were brought to the notice of the public in one way or another: *Alexander's Feast* (B.B.C.) January 1937; *Saul* (stage performance) Cambridge, February 1937; *Susanna* (stage performance) Cambridge, November 1937; and others, as listed more fully later on.

Handel non può mia musa, *Apollo e Dafne* and *La Resurrezione* were given in a series of special recitals of oratorios and cantatas under the title *Handel in Rome*, by the B.B.C., April 11–23, 1938. The first two recitals were conducted by Anthony Lewis, the third consisting of *La Resurrezione*, translated and conducted by Julian Herbage, was the first performance of this work in England. Anthony Lewis also conducted a performance of *Apollo and*

Daphne, with English translation by Geoffrey Dunn on August 11, 1938. *Acis and Galatea* was televised on May 3, 1938.

A significant event was a full-scale opera production of *Rodelinda* at The Old Vic on June 5, 1939, by the Department of Arts of Dartington Hall (Dartington Hall Opera Group), the work being repeated on June 14, 16 and 17. It was the first performance of a Handel opera I had seen and I remember the deep impression it made upon me.

The renaissance of Handel in England had commenced, and from then on until the present time keener interest in the composer and the desire for a fuller knowledge of his lesser known works have been apparent in the many productions and performances that have been given, and the great amount of literature in books, pamphlets and articles that has been published, as recorded later on.

With the idea of celebrating Handel's two-hundred-and-fiftieth anniversary The Handel Society, founded by Lord Balfour in 1882, sent out in 1935 an appeal for new members, and also for support for a performance of *Belshazzar*. But after a performance of *Joshua* at The Royal College of Music in May 1939 the Society ceased to function – a regrettable end – and there was no longer a Handel Society in England until the formation of the Deal and Walmer Handelian Society in 1946.

8

HANDEL'S FIRST SONG
ON THE LONDON STAGE –
HIS HOUSE – HANDEL THE MAN

MOST HANDELIANS know something about Handel's practice of using the compositions of other musicians in his own works, and also his use of his own material for more than one work. The standard book on this subject, probably long out of print and not well known today, is Sedley Taylor's *The Indebtedness of Handel to Works by Other Composers. A Presentation of the Evidence* (Cambridge University Press, 1906.) It is a revealing book, but the author omitted one example worth mentioning – the use of the Aria "Hò un non sò che nel cor" for three different works. The story is fully told by me in "Handel's First Song on the London Stage" (*Music and Letters*, October 1935, pp. 286–292) so it is unnecessary to do more than briefly refer to it here. The aria first appeared in the Oratorio *La Resurrezione*, Rome, 1708, where it was given to Maddalena (as Streatfeild says, "A graceful little song expressing Mary Magdalene's joy in her Saviour's resurrection"). It then appeared with slight variations in Handel's opera *Agrippina*, where it was sung in the title role by Signora Margherita Durastanti. Signor Boschi and his wife were in the cast of *Agrippina* and it may have been through them that the aria was brought to England and sung in A. Scarlatti's *Pirro e Demetrio*, London, December 6, 1710, as "The Famous Mock Song, to 'Ho un non so che nel cor'", commencing "Good folks come here I'll sing". The number is not included in the contemporary Walsh issues of *Pyrrhus and Demetrius*, but in *The Monthly Mask of Vocal Musick*, May 1711. The tune also appeared as two different sheet songs beginning "In Kent so fam'd of old", and "Tis not y^r wealth my Dear", and in various publications, *The Merry Musician*, etc. The last use of it by Handel, who must have liked it very much, was in the 1734 revival of *Il Pastor Fido*, with the original text. To round off this brief summary of the history of the song, Sir Thomas Beecham used the tune as a Hornpipe in his Suite, "The Great Elopement".

Handel's House, 25 Brook Street, Mayfair, still stands to-day in a fine state of preservation, although the front and interior have been reconstructed since the composer lived there. It is occupied by business firms and has a commemorative plaque on the front. From time to time it has been suggested that the house should be acquired by private or public funds and kept as a Handel Museum. I remember that many years ago Newman Flower had ideas of buying it, and using part of it as a flat for himself, but the price suggested made it impossible. In February, 1937, a scheme was launched and a committee formed to raise funds for acquiring the property for a museum, but in spite of appeals and announcements in the Press and elsewhere the response was negligible, and collapsed after a fairly successful concert at Crosby Hall in February 1938, conducted by Hubert Langley, had produced £50 or so for the fund.

Concurrent with the Handel House Scheme Major Benton Fletcher, who lived in the Old Devonshire House, 48 Devonshire Street, Bloomsbury, and had a fine collection of harpsichords and other instruments (now in Fenton House, Hampstead) suggested that his premises and collection might very well be the home and nucleus of a Handel Museum. He put out an appeal for that purpose, but nothing came of it. The house was destroyed during the War – the contents having fortunately been removed to safety elsewhere.

I attended the Crosby Hall concert, and returned home to go to bed with the worst form of pneumonia and a temperature of 106 degrees which lasted a number of days. I was not expected to live, but in the providence of God, with the help of a good doctor and the unremitting care and nursing of my dear wife I was spared, as I felt at the time, with something still to do in the world.

It was during this illness that two signal honours were conferred upon me – The Handel Medal from the City of Halle, and the Honorary Freedom of the Worshipful Company of Musicians, London. I was very gratified at these two unexpected appreciations of my Handel work, and I was equally surprised and pleased when I received a Handel prize and another medal from Halle in 1961.

I was asked in 1939 to contribute an article for the *Deutsch-Englische Kulturaustausch, Halle*.[1] This was published with a German translation in *Land der Mitte. Eine Festschrift zur 50-Jahrfeier der Hallische Nachrichten* (March 21, 1939), which contained a full page reproduction of a portrait of Hitler – "Adolf Hitler, der Begründer des Grossdeutschen Reiches". This caption was followed by an extract from a speech of Hitler's in Munich, October 13, 1933:

> "Ein Volk sind wir, ein Reich wollen wir sein. So fanatisch wie für die Grösse dieses Reiches, für seinen Frieden, aber auch für seine Ehre eintreten, so wenig wir dulden, dass irgendein Geist der Zwietracht die Einheit der Nation bedroht, unverständige Eigenbrötelei die Kraft des politischen Willens schwäche, so sehr hängen wir an der Eigenart der deutschen Lande und wollen pflegen den Reichtum der Vielgestaltigkeit unseres inneren Lebens."[2]

Empty words when we remember to what depths Hitler and his associates dragged Germany down. The language is strangely like much that I heard and read in East Germany from 1955 onwards.

My article "Handel – The Man" was included in *Concerning Handel*, and the last paragraph reads: "As an Englishman I am proud and very pleased to be allowed to contribute this inadequate attempt at a portrait of one of Germany's greatest sons,

---

[1] "Handel – The Man".
[2] For English translation, see p. 154.

who became an honoured British subject. It is to the lasting credit of the two nations that the Country of his birth and the Country of his adoption find in his work and life a bond of mutual friendship."

I did not know at the time that I should visit the Halle Handel Festivals from 1955 onwards, or that the above paragraph was practically the text on which I would speak so many times in the composer's birthplace – the mutual bond of Handel overriding national, political and religious barriers – and I have plenty of evidence that the East German people generally agreed with me. In fact, when I was honoured in 1961 by the gift of the City of Halle's Handel Prize, the accompanying citation said that I had made a substantial contribution towards achieving a close cultural co-operation between the English and the German peoples in the spirit of George Frideric Handel.

9

THE NATIONAL LIBRARY OF SCOTLAND HANDEL COLLECTION – THE PAUL HIRSCH COLLECTION

ONE OF THE finest collections of early editions of Handel's music and libretti of the operas and oratorios is in the National Library of Scotland, Edinburgh. This is the famous collection which belonged to that enthusiastic Handelian, Julian Marshall. Its whereabouts after his death was not generally known even to Handelians, but it had been bought by Arthur J. Balfour, afterwards Earl Balfour, and kept at his house at Whittingehame, Haddington, Scotland. After his death it went to Viscount Traprain, now Earl Balfour.

In November 1937 he visited me at the British Museum in order to discuss the question of the disposal of the collection, as he was not personally very interested in the subject, but said he would like it to go if possible to a public institution. I laughingly made him a sporting offer for it – which I advised him to refuse, and pointed out that this famous collection, formerly owned by a famous Scotsman should go to a Scottish Institution. I told him that I thought that, subject to arrangement about valuation and price, the National Library of Scotland might like to acquire it. I put Viscount Traprain and myself in touch with Dr. H. W. Meikle, Librarian of the National Library of Scotland, and by March 1938 the transaction was completed and this historic collection found its right and permanent home in Edinburgh. There it has been beautifully housed and carefully catalogued on the spot, and all the musical items are separately listed in my *Handel Catalogue* (1960) in so far as they come within the period and purpose of that work. Charles Humphries and I visited the National Library when I was preparing my catalogue, and we were struck with the efficient arrangements for our working there and the great assistance we had from Miss Marion Linton, M.A., the competent and helpful Music Librarian.

In 1948 the National Library staged an exhibition of fifty-one Handel items during the Edinburgh Musical Festival of that year, and I was privileged to write the introduction to the Catalogue of the Exhibition.

The British Museum, with the assistance of special grants from the Treasury and the Pilgrim Trust, acquired in 1946 by purchase for £120,000 the library of Paul Hirsch. This is an enormous collection for any one man to have acquired and was formerly kept in Hirsch's beautiful house at Frankfurt-am-Main.

I knew Hirsch for a good many years. He used to come to England regularly and buy things for his collection, in the days when prices were very low. He told me how, even as a young collector, when he could hardly afford the money he was then paying for them, he felt that it was wise to acquire what items he could and never regretted it.

He issued over the years 1928–47 a sumptuous catalogue in four beautifully illustrated volumes, of which he gave me a copy. Sets of the catalogue have been listed at £75, and specially bound sets at £140. For practical purposes the Museum has issued catalogues of the music and literature in the collection at very reasonable prices, £2 2s and £2 15s respectively. The Handel section of the music consists of some seventy or so items, mostly duplicates of editions already in the Museum.

Paul Hirsch settled at Cambridge where he died in 1951. He and his magnificent library were lost to Germany through the tyrannical Nazi régime, which Hirsch clearly outwitted in getting his collection here in 1936.

10

THE GERALD COKE COLLECTION

OF PRIVATE Handel collections in England that of Gerald Coke, of Jenkyn Place, Bentley, Hants is one of the best. I first met the owner when he was a young man, and enthusiastically starting what he intended to be a library of early editions of several of the classical masters, Mozart, Bach, Handel and others. After a few years he decided to concentrate on Handel, and this he has done to very good effect. His collection includes manuscripts, early printed editions, libretti, literature and many other things – engravings, mezzotints, pictures and miscellaneous Handeliana – all beautifully housed and displayed to advantage. Gerald Coke has always most generously made his collection accessible to Handelian scholars, students and enthusiasts. He has been particularly kind and helpful to me, always being ready to find time to answer troublesome letters in detail, and I have had the great pleasure of enjoying his hospitality at Bentley and working at will on his material. Most of the early editions of Handel in the collection are listed in my *Handel Catalogue*.

Perhaps the most treasured item in the collection is a complete copy of Handel's will, and the four codicils all duly signed and witnessed. Strangely enough Handel and the other signatories all executed these documents in duplicate. Why, nobody seems to know. Here I quote from "More Handeliana", (*Music and Letters*, January 1953, pp. 15 and 16):

> "For some reason, Handel left two copies of his will, and of the four codicils. The official copy of these documents, as attested and proved April 26, 1759, is in the Principal Probate Registry, Somerset House. The other copy, after passing through various

hands, is now in the possession of Gerald Coke. The details of the will and codicils have frequently been repeated, but some questions have never been cleared up. The two copies of the will and codicils were obviously written out together at the respective times of their completion, and in each case the handwriting of the original and of the duplicate is the same. The will is in Handel's own hand; the first, second and fourth codicils are in another's; and the third codicil is in yet another and distinctly different one. The statement has been made that the first, second and fourth codicils are in the hand of Smith senior, the third probably in that of his son; but this is not so. The first, second and fourth codicils appear to be in the hand of John Hetherington (of the First Fruits Office, Middle Temple), who witnessed the first and second codicils and who is mentioned in the fourth codicil; and from an examination of his signatures and name in these documents I am pretty certain that he was the amanuensis of the first, second and fourth codicils.

"We have a clear example of J. C. Smith junior's hand in the codicil which he made to his own will, and from this it is obvious that Handel's third codicil was not written by Smith junior, whose signatures to his own will and codicil are also evidence that he and not his father (as some have wrongly stated), was one of the witnesses to Handel's last codicil.

"The only differences worth mentioning between the two wills are, first, that in Gerald Coke's copy, Handel at first wrote: 'I give and bequeath to M^r. Christopher Smith Senior my large Harpsicord' &c. and afterwards deleted 'Senior'. In the Probate copy 'Senior' does not occur at all.   Again, in Gerald Coke's copy, Handel at first wrote 'All the next and residue of my Estate in South Sea Annuity's or of what soever kind or nature, I give and bequeath unto my Dear Niece Johanna Friderica Flöerken' etc., and then amended it to read 'in Bank Annuity's.' The Probate copy gives without any alteration 'in Bank Annuity's 1746. 1st sub . . . Flöercken'. This seems fairly clear proof that the Coke copy was written out first, and it looks as if Handel was undecided whether he should leave to his niece 'South Sea Annuity's' or 'Bank Annuity's 1746. 1st sub': We know from Percy Young's interesting statement on Handel's finances, that the composer had dealings in both of these forms of stock. It may, in fact, have been about this time that he got rid of his

South Sea stock, or intended to. Is it unreasonable to suppose that Handel wrote the Coke draft of the will first, and because of alterations preferred to make a fresh copy and kept the two together; and that, when he came to make the first codicil he decided to have a duplicate also prepared? – a practice which he followed for the subsequent codicils. In the affidavit of John Du Burk, Handel's servant, April 24, 1759, filed at the Probate Registry, it is stated that he 'was present when a Search was made after his (Handel's) Death for his Will' and that the 'Will . . . hereto annext . . . with the four Codicils . . . were all found locked and sealed up together in a Cover in the said deceased's Bureau in his the deceased's late Dwelling House in Brook Street'. This obviously refers to the Probate Registry documents, and there is no mention of duplicates. Most likely George Amyand as executor and close friend, was present when the last codicil was made and it was apparent that Handel was near his end, and that Amyand took away the complete set of duplicate documents."

Further details of the legacies and legatees are to be found in the article "More Handeliana".

An office copy of the will with the four codicils, and probate documents, April 26, 1759, which formerly belonged to Handel's niece, Madame Veuve Auguste Kroll, a member of the Taust family of Halle, are in the Royal College of Music (MS. 2190) and were exhibited at the Purcell–Handel Commemorative Exhibition, British Museum, May–August, 1959.

The manuscripts in the Coke Collection include:

Two small autograph items: Leaf of an unpublished Prelude. First two bars of the Allegro, Suite in B flat, Vol. II, No. 1.

Scores and in some cases parts or extracts only, various dates, of:

Oratorios: *Acis and Galatea*; *Alexander's Feast*, score and instrumental parts; *L'Allegro il Penseroso ed il Moderato*, Aylesford ms. and another; *Athalia*, 2 mss., 1764, 1850; *Esther*, 2 mss.; *Hercules; Joseph*, Aylesford ms.; *Joshua*, Earl of Shaftesbury's copy; *Messiah*, 2 mss., 3 vols.; see *Musical Opinion*, April 1958, p. 463; 2 vols. German ms.; *Samson*, Samuel Arnold's copy; *Song (Ode) for St. Cecilia's Day*.

Operas: *Admetus; Agrippina,* full score and eighteen separate songs; *Alexander; Amadis,* full score; *Amadigi,* 1715 and ten songs; *Ariadne; Arminius; Atalanta; Julius Cæsar,* vocal score owned by T. W. Taphouse and A. H. Mann with notes by Mann; *Muzio Scevola,* "Fine del Atto. Sig^r Handel 1721"; *Orlando,* overture in seven parts; *Porus,* overture, harpsichord; *Radamistus,* aires in four parts, strings and aria "Sommi Dei"; *Rinaldo,* additional songs; see *Musical Times,* April, 1937, pp. 312–14; *Teseo,* 2 mss., full score and overture; two volumes of Songs from *Teseo, Radamistus, Flavius, Parthenope, Porus* and *Sosarme.*

Miscellaneous: Italian Duets and Cantatas; 7 Anthems; Chandos Te Deum; Dettingen Te Deum; Instrumental Music including an unpublished Sonatina; 4 volumes of Handel Songs; 6 volumes of Songs some by Handel; 10 Notebooks of Songs and Instrumental Music some by Handel; set of 9 Instrumental Parts, some Handel.

Other items of special note in the collection are:

Autograph receipt for Kettledrums, etc. January 18, 1738–9.

Two copies of the first edition of the libretto of *Messiah,* Dublin, 1742.

Extra illustrated copy of the *Anecdotes of George Frederick Handel and John Christopher Smith,* 1799. (Usually attributed without evidence to William Coxe. See Smith, "Handeliana", *Music and Letters,* January 1953, pp. 11–12). This volume includes the drawing of the Music Hall, Fishamble Street, Dublin (by F. W. Fairholt, c. 1840) and a receipt signed by Handel for a Dividend of the South Sea Company, March 13, 1715, and many other interesting items.

The portrait of J. C. Smith, the younger, painted by Zoffany. (See *Anecdotes of George Frederick Handel,* etc.)

A Terra Cotta model by Roubiliac for the Handel Monument in Westminster Abbey. (See *The Musical Times,* February 1961, p. 84.)

Bronze Bust of Handel. (See John Mallet, *Burlington Magazine,* April 1962.)

Portrait of John Beard by Thomas Hudson.

A typescript with many alterations and notes by George Bernard Shaw of a Causerie on Handel which he wrote for *La Revue*

Musicale, which was published April 15, 1913. There is a French translation as well as the English original and both have a number of Ms. alterations and amendments by Shaw.

Conducting score of *Alexander's Feast* dated in Ms. 1739, Walsh edition with Ms. copies of the various concertos referred to in the libretto inserted at the correct places.

Complete manuscript of *Handel. A Documentary Biography*, by Otto Erich Deutsch, which includes a lot of information not published in the book.

A small collection of manuscripts dealing with Dr. Charles Burney and Handel, including a letter from Dr. Johnson to Burney, dated September 4, 1784, concerning the dedication "To the King", which Johnson wrote for Burney's *An Account of the Musical Performances ... 1784, in Commemoration of Handel*, London, 1785. The letter was included in R. W. Chapman's *The Letters of Samuel Johnson*, Oxford, 1952, (No. 1004) where the part which Fanny Burney crossed out in the Coke manuscript has been deciphered and printed.

II

THE WILLIAM C. SMITH COLLECTION

HANDLING THE VARIOUS early editions of Handel's works, I began to feel that I would like to own a specimen or so in addition to the literature of the subject I was collecting. Prices were steadily going up. Two or three collectors in this country, besides Flower, Coke, and others in America, were making copies exceedingly scarce, and with my very modest salary I could hardly hope to obtain much more than an item or two.

I remember how in 1934 I toyed with the idea of buying a first edition of *Acis and Galatea*, and having bought it for £1 11s 6d casually announced the fact to my good wife, who never questioned how I spent the little money I could afford on personal things. She was very competent at handicrafts, and her little dip into the modest family exchequer went in that direction. But she did not, any more than I, realize that this purchase of *Acis and Galatea* was the thin end of the wedge, and that I should never again be able to refuse a Handel item offered to me that I really wanted if I could scrape up the money to buy it with.

To-day my modest collection contains some two hundred and sixty first and early editions (including perhaps the best range of early issues of *Messiah* in the country), which to-day are worth many times the price they cost me. I hope this will encourage any young enthusiast to start collecting, according to his fancy, any literary or musical rarities that he may be interested in. They will be a good investment if he really studies the subject. He will find growing pleasure in the pursuit, and I hope he will have – what I have had – "Collector's Luck", the joy of a real find over and over again. Whenever I went on holidays, or at any other time,

I visited the local booksellers and antiquarian dealers on the hunt for Handeliana, and it is surprising how generally disinterested in music they were. In recent years their attitude has changed and to-day most second-hand music dealers list their items with more care and accuracy than they did a decade or two ago. A number of specialists in musical bibliography and musicology now rival one another to obtain stocks at public sales, or by private treaty, and the catalogues that they issue are important source books for the collector and student. In my young days at the Museum, practically the only specialist second-hand music dealers in London were William Reeves of Charing Cross Road, and Ellis of Bond Street, although a number of other first-class general dealers in books, like Quaritch, Dobell, Leighton, Maggs and Elkin Mathews, issued catalogues containing music items from time to time. But in 1919 Harold Reeves, son of William, established his own business at 210 Shaftesbury Avenue, which soon became recognized as the best business of its kind in London.

I became acquainted with Harold Reeves, both in an official and private capacity, and this acquaintance soon developed into friendship. He and his good wife worked very hard to extend the business, and to give personal service to anyone interested in music. His quiet, genial and smiling personality will be recalled by those who, like myself, dropped in frequently for a chat, even when unable to afford any purchases. To him I owed a good deal, as he was always ready to show me his treasures behind the scenes, and to discuss problems of musical bibliography. Again and again I regretted that I was unable to buy from him in a large way; but had I done so, I don't think I would have had the joy in collecting that has been mine, as from time to time I squeezed out a pound or two from the domestic purse. Harold Reeves moved his business to Southbourne, Bournemouth, in 1939, where he continued it until he sold it to Kenneth Mummery, and retired to enjoy himself with his friends, musical interests, and fine collection of rarities that he retained for his personal delight until his death in 1961.

I could mention others in business and privately, who have

been friendly and helpful to me, particularly in the field of musical bibliography, especially in connection with Handel – Cecil Hopkinson, Percy Muir, Otto Haas, Leonard Hyman, Hugh Mellor, Percy Dobell, and the present day firm of William Reeves being only some of them.

Of two personal friends contacted through correspondence, I must make special mention. Edward Richardson of Melbourne, Australia, first wrote to me about a Handel question in May 1935. This was the beginning of what developed into a regular correspondence continuing until the present time. His letters are a delight; his musical and other cultural interests widespread, and his kindness ever to be remembered by my wife and me. During the days of food shortages he started sending us parcels from Australia, and continued to do so regularly. He will blush if he ever reads this, but I dare not say anything about friends in this record without mentioning "Eddie". His collection of music includes three Aylesford manuscripts:

"I know that my Redeemer liveth" (*Messiah*).
The Overture to *Floridante* (harpsichord).
"Pupille sdegnare" from *Muzio Scevola*.

Another enthusiastic Handelian whom I have been proud to know in recent years is Dr. James S. Hall, O.B.E., F.R.C.S., of Walmer, Kent – Founder, Chairman of the Committee and Conductor of the Deal and Walmer Handelian Society, and a keen musician, collector of Handeliana, and research worker. I will say something more about Dr. Hall and his work later on.

12

FRANK KIDSON –
BIBLIOGRAPHICAL WORKS BY
SMITH AND HUMPHRIES

I RETIRED FROM THE British Museum at the end of 1944, after 44 years of service, which was appreciated by the gift of the portrait drawing of myself from life by David Bell, which is reproduced as a frontispiece to this book. I was very happy at the Museum, but since then have found the days all too short for me to do the many things I try to do, especially to keep my research work going. It was fortunate to be able to carry on one's work as a hobby in retirement, instead of trying to take up some entirely new and unsatisfactory form of recreation.

I had in preparation my Walsh book, which eased the break from regular day-to-day work to freedom of choice and time; and there were other occupations and activities looming ahead in the shape of books I hoped to publish; the growing correspondence and association with many Handelians at home and abroad; the increasing interest in adding to my collection of Handeliana, and from 1955 the quite unexpected and absorbing visits to the Handel Festivals behind the Iron Curtain at Halle. The contacts, work and correspondence which arose out of those visits, and the fascinating personal experiences, musical and otherwise, which I had are subjects that I hope to deal with elsewhere.

Any enthusiastic student of the early editions of Handel's works will very soon find that he must take stock of the eighteenth-century publishing firm of John Walsh, and the part he and his son played in making the music accessible in printed form. Soon after I had succeeded Squire at the Museum I realized how much simpler most of the cataloguing of early music would be if there were dictionaries and bibliographies of publishers, printers and engravers, and I began to take an interest in building up what material I could, for use at some future time in one way or another.

The great problem for the cataloguer of early music is to date the copies. Most music of the eighteenth century is not dated, and therefore accurate or approximate dates, very often, can be supplied only after a great deal of research in records, papers, histories, biographies; by the study of paper-making, watermarks and music printing; in directories and other probable sources. This was the problem that faced Squire when he started his *Catalogue of Printed Music*, and as I have pointed out, considering the few sources he was able to consult, his approximate dates (within the range of five years – which was then the general practice in the Department) are surprisingly accurate.

There was only one helpful book on the subject – Frank Kidson's *British Music Publishers, Printers and Engravers, etc.* (W. E. Hill & Sons, London, 1900). This is not the place to write a deservedly comprehensive account of Frank Kidson's fine contributions to musical bibliography; of his erudite editions of old music, especially collections of songs, dances, ballad operas, etc., and of his pioneer work on music publishers, printers and engravers. He was a musical antiquary with a sound knowledge of the subjects he dealt with, and his publications are reliable and scholarly. A considerable portion of his library, including a manuscript index of airs in fifty-seven volumes, and various other manuscript catalogues, is in the Mitchell Library, Glasgow. (*Grove's Dictionary of Music and Musicians*, fifth edition, 1954, vol. IV, pp. 748–9; *Journal of the English Folk Dance and Song Society*, vol. V, No. 3, December 1948, pp. 127–35.)

In 1908 Squire gave me a copy of Kidson's *British Music Publishers*, to which I added supplementary material as it came to me in the course of my work as I searched the newspapers and other records for information. I took a particular interest in the frequently occurring name of the firm of John Walsh, senior and junior, and started a special study of their output and methods of working, which was further forced on me as I attempted from time to time to unravel the tangled skein of problems connected with the early editions of Handel. Ultimately, with the help of my colleague at the Museum, Charles Humphries, most of the eighteenth-century newspapers were searched for advertisements of the publications of Walsh and other firms, and special notice was taken of references to publications of works by Handel and performances of them.

The direct results from this research were, first of all the correction of many of the dates in Squire's *Catalogue*; then the preparation of my *Bibliography of the Musical Works published by John Walsh during the years 1695–1720* (Bibliographical Society, London, 1948); and the gathering together of an enormous amount of material on Handel and his works, without which it would have been impossible for me to publish my *Handel. A Descriptive Catalogue of the Early Editions* (Cassell, London, 1960), and various articles I have written.

The newspaper notices of publishers other than Walsh were valuable material for *Music Publishing in the British Isles* (Humphries and Smith, Cassell, London, 1954), and of considerable help when I was contributing to or editing articles on the subject for *Grove's Dictionary of Music and Musicians*, fifth edition. I and Humphries have prepared for publication a successor to my *Walsh Bibliography*, carrying on the history of the firm from 1721–66, and Dr. James S. Hall of Walmer, Kent, has accumulated a great amount of original material about John Walsh, senior and junior, which should be published.

13

DR. JAMES S. HALL, HIS COLLECTION, AND THE DEAL AND WALMER HANDELIAN SOCIETY

MY FIRST Handel book was *Concerning Handel, His life and works* (Cassell & Co., 1948), and consists of eight essays – some having been published previously. It was generally well received, and I felt happy about it on the whole.

Among the correspondents who wrote about the book was Dr. James S. Hall, mentioned above. In a letter to me dated June 2, 1950, he said: "I wanted to write directly to you about three things. First, to thank you for *Concerning Handel*, which I am re-reading for about the sixth time", . . . He also enclosed photographic facsimiles of a title page of an early edition of *Acis and Galatea* and one of *Israel in Egypt*.

This was the beginning of a correspondence, acquaintance, and soon a close friendship with one of the great Handelians of to-day. An eminent surgeon and physician with a busy professional practice, he has found time for an extraordinary amount of work on Handel; the performing of the oratorios, and the building up of the largest collection of Handel's music in the British Isles outside the public libraries and institutions. The significant feature about his library, in addition to the early editions, libretti, literature, facsimiles, recordings and other things it includes, is the large collection of the Novello nineteenth-century vocal scores of the composer's works. These Dr. Hall has collected over the years from booksellers and other sources whenever they came to his notice. As these editions – now out of print – were the ones usually used in the nineteenth century, and indeed, in the case of most of them, until to-day for performances of the oratorios and other works, Dr. Hall has provided a great service for conductors and choirs by being able to supply them on loan with twenty, thirty, forty, fifty or more copies of works they wish to perform; and consignments of copies are continually going from Walmer to many places in England and America!

Dr. Hall has been extremely kind to me in many ways, and very helpful. Everything that he thinks may be of interest to me in my work he gives me notice of, and in many cases supplies photostats. I am always at liberty to stay with him and his family and range at will over his fine collection, which is well catalogued and easy of access. He is an indefatigable research worker, and in addition to the articles on Handelian and kindred subjects, and a small biography of the composer (Boosey & Hawkes, 1961), will be remembered for his medical services during the war – delightfully told in *Sea Surgeon*, (William Kimber, 1960) – and for which he was awarded the O.B.E. He has gathered together much material on J. C. Smith, father and son, and was influential in the placing of a commemorative plaque on the house in Carlisle Street, Soho, London, where the elder Smith lived. This was unveiled on April 21, 1958, by Sir Charles Norton, Mayor of Westminster, in the presence of His Excellency the Ambassador of the German Federal Republic. Dr. Hall was also responsible for the placing of a plaque on the house in Brock Street, Bath, where the younger Smith lived. This plaque was unveiled on October 11, 1954, by Frank Howes, C.B.E. A plaque was also placed on the site in Dublin where the first performance of *Messiah* was given in 1742. This was unveiled by Dr. Hall on October 5, 1959, who afterwards opened a Handel Exhibition in the Civic Museum, Dublin, arranged by the Music Association of Ireland.

Another example of the ceaseless activity of this indefatigable doctor was the microfilming, transcribing, translating and type-scripting of the catalogue of the huge Schœlcher collection of Handel material in the Bibliothèque Nationale, Paris. Except for the manuscript catalogue in the King's Music Library (RM.18. b.2) and some other references, nothing was available in detail about the Paris Collection until Dr. Hall produced his copy of the complete catalogue with the help of William B. West, of Deal, Kent. I am the proud possessor of the four volumes of the catalogue – a present from Dr. Hall – and the information contained in them is an amazing contribution to any full scale study of the composer and his works – much of it unobtainable elsewhere. Incidentally, Dr. Hall does his own typing, photostating and bookbinding.

The Deal and Walmer Handelian Society, founded by Dr. Hall in 1946, has performed the following works by the Composer: *Acis and Galatea, Alexander's Feast, Belshazzar, The Choice of Hercules, Coronation Anthems, Deborah, Dettingen Te Deum, Israel in Egypt, Jephtha, Joshua, Judas Maccabæus, L'Allegro ed il Penseroso, Messiah, Ode for St. Cecilia's Day, Samson, Saul, Brockes Passion, Solomon, Utrecht Jubilate, Ways of Zion* (Funeral Anthem), *O praise the Lord with one consent* (Chandos Anthem); and in addition they have performed works by J. S. Bach, Borodin, Britten and other composers. This is a remarkable record for a small amateur Society in a small town.

For the performance of *L'Allegro ed il Penseroso* in April 1958, Dr. Hall was able to arrange for the personal appearance of Philine Fischer, the Prima Donna of the Halle Theatre in East Germany, and the creator of many Handelian roles there. It was a very much appreciated gesture on the part of Philine Fischer to learn her part in English for this small amateur group, and her brilliant singing and interpretation created a deep impression on all who heard her.

A pleasing after event was the visit in 1959 of the Society to Halle, where the work was given again under Dr. Hall's direction, with Philine Fischer, Rolf Apreck and Kurt Hübenthal from Halle in addition to Eileen Rickon, from London, as soloists, and with the Staatliches Sinfonieorchester, Halle. A second performance was broadcast by the Halle and Berlin Radio Stations. Dr. Hall's articles on *Messiah* problems are listed later on.

14

"MESSIAH" – INTERPRETATION AND PERFORMANCE – PUBLICATIONS 1946–64

IN ADDITION TO what has already been said about *Messiah* and interpretations of the work, it is necessary to mention some recent attempts to throw new light on the subject, about which many questions are still unanswered.

The principal problems confronting the editor or conductor of the work are: which manuscripts and printed editions are the most authoritative; which alternative versions of arias, etc. did Handel prefer; how should the music itself as it appears in the manuscripts be interpreted; what is the correct figured bass – and other technical points. It is not intended to discuss such questions here, and I have not the musical knowledge to do so. There are, however, one or two points that should be raised before calling attention to the work of some special editors and writers on the subject of *Messiah* that must be consulted.

Some of the definite statements made about manuscripts and editions appear to me to be open to question. For instance, the "Dublin" score at Tenbury has been accepted by Watkins Shaw and others as the copy used by the composer for the first performances in Dublin, but there are some questions that arise in connection with it.

First of all, is it reasonable to suppose that Handel needed a fair copy to conduct from the harpsichord? If so, can we identify copies of his other works that he used in the same way? Some may have been kept with the orchestral parts at the theatres and were lost when those buildings were destroyed by fire.

Secondly, the "Dublin" manuscript is obviously without certain numbers that previously existed in the same copyist's hand, in place of which certain autograph pages have been inserted.

Thirdly, if it was the composer's performing copy, careful as he was he would hardly have allowed the manuscript to disappear from his collection unless it was kept with other fair copies at the Theatre, as mentioned above.

Fourthly, we know nothing definite of its history until it turned up in the sale room in 1838 – being sold for one guinea to "Warner". The sale catalogue description was:

> "Dublin Score. Sacred Music. Handel's *Messiah*, with alterations and adaptations, in the autograph of the Author. To the admirers of Handel this volume is one of the highest interest, having been used by its celebrated author in the production of his oratorio in Dublin, whither the intrigues of his rivals and enemies in England had driven him to resort for the production of his masterpiece; on which occasion the corrections and alterations in question were made by himself."

The statements of Rockstro in his *Life of G. F. Handel*, p. 245, in the British Museum Handel Exhibition Catalogue, 1951, and also by Canon Fellowes (*Tenbury Catalogue*) about the history of the manuscript before the sale in 1838, appear to be speculative without any real evidence, although it is probable that it was once in the collection which passed to J. C. Smith and his son, from which it was subsequently separated at some unknown date. It is impossible to record here the arguments about, and the evidence for, the various opinions of Handelian authorities on this manuscript, which is of unquestioned importance, even if we do not know its real history.

An interesting question also arises in connection with the Foundling Hospital Score and Parts, said to be those given to the Hospital under Handel's will. In 1896, one hundred and thirty-seven years after his death, they were discovered there by Henry Davon Wetton, the organist. I have sometimes wondered whether these are the ones presented two months after Handel's death, in accordance with the codicil to his will (August 4, 1757), or whether they may be another set of a manuscript score and thirty-five vocal and instrumental parts sold at Puttick & Simpson's in January 1858.

The subject of figured bass in the various early editions has been dealt with in my *Handel Catalogue*. It is referred to again here as another problem for the experts.

On March 18, 1950, John Tobin, conductor of the London Choral Society, gave in St. Paul's Cathedral the first of his performances of an edition of *Messiah* based on his own research and conclusions about how the work should be performed, instrumented and, in particular, ornamented. Since then he has worked indefatigably at the subject, giving performances at the Royal Festival Hall every year – most of which I attended, including the first at St. Paul's Cathedral which created enormous public interest, ten thousand applying for admission.

No one can question the zeal and energy with which Tobin has gone into every one of the early manuscripts and editions in order to justify his conclusions and interpretations of the work, but as can be expected, his version evoked a good deal of criticism and correspondence in the musical journals. He has, to my personal knowledge, never ceased his studies on this absorbing subject, and it is to be hoped that his edition of *Messiah*, which he has prepared for publication by the Halle Handel Society, will soon be available. One thing he has done is to banish for ever the idea that we can just take Handel, as existing in some of the accepted versions, for granted, but must bring to the study of the subject the best musicianship, technical knowledge and research. His scholarly notes in his *Messiah* programmes, and his contributions to the musical journals on the subject are invaluable. To my knowledge he is the only editor of *Messiah* who has consulted in detail the copy of the earliest known Walsh edition, which is in my library.

The following extracts from the notes in the 1950 and 1961 *Messiah* programmes by John Tobin give some idea of his new

6

approach to the subject and what he was endeavouring to do:

"This performance is not for the musicologist alone. It is not simply an attempt to perform *Messiah* 'as Handel wrote it', (except in so far as it is free from many textual errors and un-Handelian 'improvements' of various editors). It is an attempt to regain something of the Chamber Music quality of performance for which Handel conceived the work: the lightness of texture; intensity rather than volume; the timbre and percussive quality of the harpsichord, and the style of elaborate decoration necessary at times in playing an instrument relatively weak in volume and sustaining power; the colour of the orchestral sound – the mixture of string and reed tone and the brilliance of the original high trumpet parts; the conventions of performance – the intention behind the written symbol – the use of appoggiature and vocal ornamentation in general.

"The custom of ornamenting the melody is as ancient as music; but in considering the ornamentation in *Messiah* it is necessary to remember that Handel's style was essentially Italian; and Italian composers in the middle of the eighteenth century were beginning to follow the French custom of writing in full whatever ornament they desired, be it a simple appoggiatura or an elaborate mixture of nachschlag, slide and prall-triller. There is however little doubt that a certain discretion was allowed the performer." (March 18, 1950.)

"Very soon after Handel's death alterations in the musical text of *Messiah* and in style and scale of performance began to be made and these have grown into a tradition so that, although *Messiah* has continued to be performed, it is not *Handel's Messiah*. In fact to perform the Oratorio as it will be heard in this performance, with the instrumental and choral balance, in the style and with the text including alternative versions, as it was performed under Handel's own direction, is tantamount to presenting a new work." ...

"As a result the Oratorio has been swept and garnished in text and texture – swept free of textual errors and additional un-Handelian orchestration, and garnished by the conventions of eighteenth-century performance which were an essential part of Handel's conception of the work. This together with the chamber music style of performance, lightness of texture, intensity rather than volume and the instrumental colour and at times elaborate decoration of the harpsichord reveals afresh the whole musical structure of the Oratorio". . . .

"To this appoggiatura-starved generation vocal ornamentation reeks of bad taste if not of outright vulgarity. But a study of musical performance during the seventeenth and eighteenth centuries proves that composers wrote their music with a view to its being ornamented, often quite elaborately. True it has to be done tastefully, but done it must be." . . .

"Accordingly I have decorated both the orchestral accompaniment and the vocal line." (May 6, 1961.)

Important publications by John Tobin are:

> *Messiah* restored – An Apologia. (*Musical Times*, April 1950, pp. 133–134.)
> A New *Messiah* Manuscript. (*Musical Times*, October, 1961, pp. 627–30.)
> A *Messiah* Problem. (*Music and Letters*, October, 1955, pp. 357–64.)
> *The Messiah*. (*I.S.M. Music Journal*, vol. 27, No. 2, October, 1961, pp. 16–17.)
> Handel at Work. (Handel's first, second and third thoughts as disclosed in his many alterations in the Autograph Manuscripts of *Messiah*.) Cassell & Co., 1964.

In addition to his *Messiah* performances in London, John Tobin has also given the oratorio at the International Eisteddfod at Llangollen, Wales (July 12, 1959) and performances in London of *Alexander Balus* (May 8, 1952), *Ode for St. Cecilia's Day* (June 1, 1951) and *Samson* (February 28, 1959).

Another contemporary editor and investigator into the problems of *Messiah* is H. Watkins Shaw, Senior Lecturer (Music) at the City of Worcester Training College, and Honorary Librarian of St. Michael's College, Tenbury Wells. Like John Tobin, he has been working during the same time over much the same sources and material, with an equal zeal for the facts, and has published some articles and pamphlets. His conclusions and practice can fortunately be studied in his edition of the vocal score of the oratorio (Novello & Co., 1958), to which *A Textual Companion* is to be published in due course. *Handel's "Messiah" the story of a Masterpiece*, by H. Watkins Shaw (Hinrichsen, London, 1946) is an informative booklet of "useful facts and certain opinions" about Handel's great work, with an "Appendix: Sources of the musical text". It is of particular interest as it raises in advance a number of problems dealt with later by John Tobin and others. His conclusions are:

> "*Messiah* has suffered from its universal popularity . . .
>
> "*Messiah* has yet to have lavished upon it the loving care and preparation that have become a feature of the Bach cult . . .
>
> "*Messiah* needs a crusader's campaign . . . It is indeed a fine thing that the mass of the people have yielded to the spell of music such as this. Let it therefore have the care, scholarship and respect due to a noble creation of a great mind."

Other important contributions to the subject by Shaw are:

A London performance of *Messiah* in 1767. (*Musical Opinion*, January 1958, pp. 245, 247, 249.)

John Matthew's manuscript of *Messiah*. (*Music and Letters*, April 1958, pp. 101–117.)

Covent Garden performances of *Messiah* in 1749, 1752 and 1753. (*Music Review*, May 1958, pp. 85–93.)

A Handelian team of *Messiah* singers; 1749 or 1750? (*Monthly Musical Record*, September–October 1958, pp. 169–73.)

Handel's *Messiah*: a study of selected contemporary word-books. (*Musical Quarterly*, April 1959, pp. 208–22.)

A First List of word-books of Handel's *Messiah*, 1742–83, pp. 20. Printed for the Author . . . Worcester [1959].

Thoughts on editing *Messiah* – an informal discourse. (*Musical Opinion*, March 1958, pp. 401, 403, 405; April 1958, pp. 461, 463.)

Messiah. St. Martin-in-the-Fields, London. (Introductory note to Programme, December 8, 1959.)

Handel's Conducting Score of *Messiah*. (St. Michael's College, Tenbury Wells, 1962, pp. 8.)

An inaccessible *Messiah* Manuscript. (*Music Review*, May 1962, pp. 109–118.)

The "Sterndale Bennett" Manuscript Score of *Messiah*. (*Music and Letters*, April 1963, pp. 118–122.)
The Story of Handel's *Messiah* 1741–1784. pp. 79. Novello, London, 1963.

In the 'thirties I first made the acquaintance of J. M. Coopersmith (now Doctor), who had a travelling scholarship to Europe in order to visit libraries, collections and musical scholars for the preparation of special studies on the Handel manuscripts, editions, libretti, pictures, etc., to gather material for a Thematic Catalogue of the Composer's works, and to list hitherto unpublished or unknown manuscripts. He was then a very enthusiastic young man and I was amazed at his zeal and knowledge. Since then he has contributed articles on Handel to various journals, but his great *Thematic Catalogue*, which would be of tremendous use to so many Handelians is I understand, locked up in the Library of Congress, Washington, and only to be consulted on the spot. Why such a work has never been published I do not know.

Fortunately Dr. Coopersmith has given us one major work – his vocal score of *Messiah*, published by Carl Fischer, New York, 1947. It is a most original and authoritative edition, dealing very fully with problems of alternative versions of arias, technicalities, corruptions and mistakes in other versions, and details of performance, etc. – an essential addition to any collection of earlier scores. The following are extracts from Dr. Coopersmith's Preface:

"The frequency of performance during Handel's own lifetime necessitated alterations in the work, which in some instances were merely transpositions for new singers; while, in others, they represent a reworking of the musical structure to accomodate a redisposition of the voices. To meet the needs of certain other performances, Handel made several excisions which called for a new setting of the text. The present edition contains not only the work as it is usually performed, but also every known variant of the separate excerpts." . . .

"The problems of vocal ornamentation not only in Handel's works, but also in the whole body of early eighteenth-century music require further clarification. Preliminary studies of some importance have been made by Max Seiffert and Hugo Goldschmidt. That a very specialized type of ornamentation was common in Handel's time must be accepted in principle. Unfortunately, the few examples that have survived do not permit conclusive systematization. In the large mass of Handel's vocal material, the editor has found only one instance of added ornamentation in autograph: the aria, 'Benchè mi sia crudele', from the opera *Ottone*. To this example may now be added three others, all in the handwriting of John Christopher Smith, Handel's amanuensis. . . . Even the survival of this small group would seem to indicate that ornamentation was a common practice, that it differed with each singer, and finally, that it was seldom written into the music except for an inexperienced vocalist."

Julian Herbage, referred to elsewhere in this work published an attractive and well illustrated small book, *Messiah* (Max Parrish & Co., London, 1948), gathering together for the first time in this way much interesting material. It concludes:

"In *Messiah* Handel has found music worthy to express the eternal verities, worthy indeed to form their eternal expression. 'Comfort ye' – the very first words – becomes the operational theme of the whole work. The story is vividly illustrated. The people that walked in darkness, the shepherds abiding in the fields, the knowledge that the Redeemer lives, despite His being despised and rejected of men – all are unforgettably portrayed. And the choruses, from the revelation of the Glory of the Lord to the Hallelujah and final Amen, give a sense of true majesty that music has never surpassed before or since. 'Art', again to quote Tolstoy, 'is not a pleasure, a solace or an amusement; art is a great matter. Art is an organ of human life, transmitting man's reasonable perception into feeling. In our age the common religious perception of men is the consciousness of the brotherhood of man – we know that the well-being of man lies in union with his fellow men.' No art could achieve this ideal more surely than Handel's music to *Messiah*. And no art is more necessary for us to-day."

In *The Oratorios* ("Handel – A Symposium", O.U.P., 1954,

pp. 95, 96) Julian Herbage says this about *Messiah*:

"The selection of the words of *Messiah* is a remarkable achievement, reflecting the humanistic spirit of the age rather than conventional religious dogma. Though its Scriptural text deals with the prophecy, birth, crucifixion and teachings of our Lord, it possesses a universal spirit that raises it above the letter of doctrine. Its message is summarized in the words which Jennens sent to Handel as an introduction to the first printed word-book of the oratorio: 'And without controversy, great is the mystery of Godliness; God was manifested in the Flesh, justified by the Spirit, seen of Angels, preached among the Gentiles, believed on in the World, received up in glory. In whom are hid all the treasures of wisdom and knowledge.'

"Thus the Gospel story is related, not by a theatrical narrative, as in the Passion oratorios, but on a metaphysical plane. For some, this places it outside the category of a truly religious work; for others, it possesses the universal essence of true religious aspiration. For Handel, it provided an epic canvas on which to paint the hope, suffering, faith, and brotherhood of his own spiritual world. If his music occasionally presents us with the pomp of kings rather than a visionary mysticism, he was merely expressing the attitude of his age towards the eternal truths of religious belief."

Among Herbage's articles on *Messiah* is one in *The Musical Times*, October 1948, pp. 297-9, "The *Messiah*. Handel's second thoughts."

Jens Peter Larsen, Professor of Musicology in the University of Copenhagen needs special mention. I first met him when he visited the British Museum just before the war, in order, I believe, to have a brief look at the Handel manuscripts in the King's Music Library, and I have had the pleasure of meeting him from time to time at the Halle Handel Festivals from 1955 onwards. His monumental work, *Handel's Messiah. Origins, Composition, Sources* (A. & C. Black, London, 1957) is an original, informative and comprehensive study by an experienced musician and musicologist, and we are fortunate that Professor Larsen published it in English in this country. His knowledge of the manuscripts is most detailed and complete, and he has surveyed every aspect of the oratorio technically and historically. He has given Handelians a work of the highest order, that in its way can never be equalled or become outdated. In dealing with the "Sources", Professor Larsen (pp. 260–303) has given us a highly technical and comprehensive study of the various hands (J. C. Smith and others) in which the manuscripts were written, with pp. 307–23 of helpful facsimiles; and in addition an equally important study of the watermarks found in the papers used by Handel and his copyists. These subjects were also dealt with by Doctor Frederick Hudson, referred to later. I am grateful to Professor Larsen for his gift to me of a copy of his invaluable book.

Other important contributions to the *Messiah* problem by Professor Larsen are:

> The Text of Handel's *Messiah*. (*Musical Quarterly*, January 1954, pp. 21–28.)
>
> Tempoprobleme bei Händel, dargestellt am *Messias*. (Händel-Ehrung der Deutschen Demokratischen Republik, Halle, April 11–19, 1959. *Konferenzbericht*, pp. 141–153. Deutscher Verlag für Musik, Leipzig, 1961.)

Dr. Percy M. Young published an informative little work: *Messiah. A study in interpretation* (Dennis Dobson, London, 1951), in which he says:

> "*Messiah* lovers may be divided into four groups. There are some actuated by a strong religious sense, who regard the oratorio as a statement of faith, as an exposition of Protestant philosophy. Others, immune from this influence and probably increasing in number, are content to regard, more or less exclusively, the musical content of a great work of art. A third group, conspicuous in choral strongholds, are conscious of a particular entertainment value, which may be enhanced by the participation of 'popular' singers. Last comes the minority, able to synthesise all these approaches, to appreciate Handel's attitude, to realise the unique quality of *Messiah* in so far as England is concerned" ... (p. 11.)
>
> "It is necessary at the outset to dismiss sentimentality. This atrocious national characteristic leads the faithful to Mr. Handel as to the vicar at a sewing meeting: unctuous effusion was as distasteful to the one as it often is to the other. In performance sanctimony

generally cloaks incompetence. Let it be dismissed. Freed from what is alleged to be a 'religious style', the performer has taken a step forward" ... (p. 12.)

"Absolute fidelity to Handelian performance is impossible. The case of the academic purist is stillborn. At the same time we can aim at coming as near to the original intentions as our resources will admit. Some latitude is clearly permissible – as in the eighteenth century. But there are frontiers which are not to be crossed." (p.14.)

This is all worth consideration and much of it can be accepted without argument; but the facts remain that *Messiah* is, was and always will be a religious work with a predominantly Protestant Evangelistic foundation, whatever entertainment value there is in it, and in their attempts "at coming as near to the original intentions" of Handel as possible, the present day editors and conductors are by no means in agreement as to what the original intentions of the composer were.

The late Robert Dalley-Scarlett, Mus.Doc., Handel Medalist, Halle, and conductor of the Brisbane Handel Society made his contribution to the subject in a little booklet, *Handel's Messiah. How can we realise the composer's intentions?* (Brisbane, 1952.) In this the author raises a number of points about interpretation, timing and versions, paying tribute to the work of Tobin, Young and others, in the course of which he says:

"My own choir, the Brisbane Handel Society, have now instituted an annual performance of Messiah complete, in Handel's style, and with Handel's timing. They realise that what they are doing is more than implementing the personal foibles of their conductor: they are carrying out the intentions of the composer, and that should be the goal of every honest and interested choir." ... (p. 21.)

"The Brisbane Handel Society intends to develop the demand for Handel's Messiah rather than A's or B's or C's until no conductor or choir will dare to revert to the old bad lumbering traction engine type of performance." (p. 22.)

It is nice to know that the "wind of change" is sweeping over the Handelian fields of "down under".

Dr. Hall has written a number of articles on *Messiah* problems, engaging spiritedly in argument with John Tobin and Watkins Shaw about their respective editions and interpretations, the most important of which are:

> The 12/8 setting of "Rejoice greatly". (*Musical Opinion*, February 1955, pp. 277, 279. This version is not generally known or used to-day.)
> A letter on John Tobin's performances. (*Music and Letters*, January 1956, pp. 98–100.)
> A letter in reply to Watkins Shaw's "A London performance of *Messiah*" in 1767. (*Musical Opinion*, March 1958, p. 419.)
> ——— A further letter. (*Musical Opinion*, May 1958, p. 545.)
> A review of Watkin Shaw's *Messiah* (Novello & Co.). (*Musical Times*, June 1959, pp. 332–3.)

An exhaustive article on ornamentation: "Handel's Graces", (Händels Verzierungen) by Dr. and Martin Hall, appeared in English and German in the *Händel-Jahrbuch* . . . 3. (IX.) *Jahrgang 1957*, pp. 25–43, 159–171, and is essential for the study of this problem which is in many respects still an open question.

Our present day better knowledge of *Messiah* is largely due to the work of Julian Herbage, John Tobin, H. Watkins Shaw, Dr. J. S. Hall, Jacob Coopersmith, Dr. Percy Young and Jens Larsen. I am proud to have known them all and have followed with particular interest their individual research work; but in addition to them many others should be remembered who are not mentioned here. The extracts from the various works given above are only a few of those that indicate the growing sense among musicians and musical scholars to-day of the importance of looking at the most popular of Handel's works with fresh minds to a new understanding of it and how it should be performed.

It is possible to mention here only a few more of the interesting modern articles on *Messiah* selected from the many that exist:

> The Text of *Messiah*. Geoffrey Cuming. (*Music and Letters*, July 1950, pp. 226–30.)

The Text of *Messiah*. William C. Smith. (*Music and Letters*, October 1950, pp. 386–7.) A comment on the previous item.

The Crooked Straight and the Rough Places Plain. Resurrecting the original *Messiah*. Jack Diether. (*Musical Opinion*, May 1958, pp. 531, 533, 535.)

Performing *The Messiah*. Richard Graves. (*Musical Times*, November 1956, pp. 588–9; January, pp. 29–30, February, pp. 84, 85, April, pp. 206–7, June, pp. 325–6, August, pp. 422–433, October, pp. 558–9, 1957. Published in pamphlet form with emendations as ,"Your performance of *Messiah*. A Guide for the amateur conductor". Novello & Co., London, 1962.)

The *Messiah* in Dublin. D. W. Kennan. (*Music Book*, vol. VII. Hinrichsen, London, 1952, pp. 460–75.)

Handel's "Messiah". A Touchstone of Taste, by Robert Manson Myers, (The Macmillan Company, New York, 1948) is an ambitious work covering many aspects of the subject historically and technically, but must be read with caution as it contains many statements open to question. The author could have made throughout more generous acknowledgement to the writers from whose work he drew much of his material that otherwise appears as the result of his own research. In this connection, while paying tribute to Kurt Taut's "Verzeichnis des Schrifttums Georg Friedrich Händel" he does not mention the foundation Bibliography in Flower's *Handel*. Pp. 179–86 of Myers's book are taken largely from "The Earliest Editions of 'Messiah' (*Concerning Handel*", pp. 67–108) with alterations and variations in the wording to suggest originality. The use of this material is hardly justified by a footnote which says that "William C. Smith has reconciled numerous contradictions and corrected traditional inaccuracies in two excellent articles: 'The Earliest Editions of Handel's *Messiah*' ... 'Handel's *Messiah*: Recent Discoveries of Early Editions'." Other characteristic instances of use of material without acknowledgment could be quoted. Nevertheless the book has in it much newly gathered information.

The problems involved in the editing, adapting and performing of Handel's works are considerable, and there is no general agreement as to how this should be done in many cases. It is rather interesting to find that some fifteen years or so after the composer's death the questions of false interpretations and adaptations were already exercising the mind of at least one purist, Robert Falkener, whose *Instructions for Playing the Harpsichord* (London, 1774) has the following introduction:

"No person can be said to be accomplished in any Art or Science unless he thoroughly understands it. Grammar, Logic, Rhetoric, Arithmetic, Geometry, Astronomy, and Music are, by way of Excellence, called the Liberal Sciences; and in the present Age none of them are more practised than Music, nor is there anything less understood. I say, less understood; because, were the present Practitioners truly instructed in the right Rules of Harmony, it would be impossible for our modern Professors to impose upon the Ears of the Public their wretched Composition, whose Parts are so poorly united, as neither to soothe Passion, raise Devotion, nor animate the Soul to courageous and daring Exploits.

"The immortal Handel, in whatever Pieces he composed for the Entertainment of the Public was extremely cautious not to admit of any thing that might excite either mean or lewd Ideas; because whenever this happens, it loses its good Effect upon the Audience, and, like bad Plays, becomes a general Evil. But the Thirst after Novelty in the present Age is so insatiable, that nothing will go down but what is new; to usher which into the World there hath not only been a total Neglect of the melodious Strains of Handel, but an indefatigable Industry in our crafty Masters to render the whole Science of Music so difficult and intricate, that scarce one in an hundred ever comes at a competent Knowledge thereof; but are led on from Lesson to Lesson, with Examples of Apogiaturas, Syncopations, Arpeggios, Mordents, Mezzo Trillos, Semitones Major and Semitones Minor, extreme Sharp Seconds and Flat Thirds, with a thousand other needless Perplexities, till tired with the Study, and sick of the Expence, they get up as ignorant of the Matter as when they sat down. Therefore, in opposition to these Darkeners of Science, and for the benefit of every rational Being, I have laid down the following Rules in as plain a Manner as I can possibly devise; wherein I have carefully avoided all superfluous Examples, and have only inserted what is necessary to form in the Mind a just Notion of

Harmony and Discord; which, if the Reader can attain, my Task is finished; he has then my free Will to enter into the most minute and trifling Degrees of Sound; and if he does not approve of the twelve half Tones in the Octave, as it stands at present, he may divide it into four and twenty, and make Instruments with Sliding Stops, etc. etc. to shew the Deficiency of former Ages, and his own consummate Abilities; In a Word, he may join Dr. Swift's Company of Academicians[1] and extract Sun-Beams from Cucumbers."

[1] See *Gulliver's Travels*, Pt. III, Ch. 5.

15

IMPORTANT BIBLIOGRAPHIES
CATALOGUES AND WORKS ON HANDEL

THE GREAT AMOUNT of Handelian literature is rather bewildering for the student, but most of the biographies have short and selected bibliographies. Mention has been made of the one in Newman Flower's biography – which was the most extensive for many years. In 1933 a much more complete bibliography, *Verzeichnis des Schrifttums über Georg Friedrich Händel*, by Kurt Taut was published in the *Händel-Jahrbuch VI*, 1933 (Breitkopf & Härtel, Leipzig) – "Veröffentlichungen der Händel-Gesellschaft Nr. 9" – in which the subjects are classified so that it is very easy to consult. A supplement to this, carried out on the same lines, extending the period covered up to 1954, by Konrad Sasse of Halle appeared in the *Händel-Jahrbuch I. (VII.)*, 1955 (Deutscher Verlag für Musik, Leipzig). A new and more complete bibliography (7,000 items) by Konrad Sasse, combining all the entries in the two previous works and supplemented by many others, was published by VEB Deutscher Verlag für Musik, 1963.

In addition to the various catalogues and other publications already mentioned, important basic contributions to Handelian literature are the four interesting items listed in the Appendix to Squire's Catalogue of the Handel Manuscripts in the King's Music Library that were added to the Collection (three by gift from Mrs. R. Carter and Miss Marshall) and which came from the library of Julian Marshall. They are as follows:

An Alphabetical Index of Italian and French Songs, etc. by

G. F. Handel. By Victor Schœlcher but not in his hand, as wrongly stated in Squire's Catalogue (RM.19.f.8). (A typescript copy of this was made by Dr. Hall, with many additions to the original list, one of the two or three copies of which are in my collection.)

"Catalogue méthodique" of the dates of composition and first performances of Handel's works; Account of the performances of Handel's Oratorios from 1732 to 1759; Lists of Handel MSS. at the British Museum, Buckingham Palace, the Fitzwilliam Museum and in the Lennard Collection; Catalogue chronological and raisonné of Handel's Works. (RM.18.b.2.) (Partly in English in the handwriting of Julian Marshall, partly in French. Probably translated, adapted or copied from Victor Schœlcher.)

Catalogue of the printed editions (excluding H.G.) of Handel's Works, and an appendix of remarks found in some volumes of Handel's works formerly in the collections of Dr. Crotch and Rophino Lacy. Autograph of Julian Marshall. (RM.18.b.1.)

G. F. Handel. Lists of (a) Original pieces in contemporary song-books or single sheets; (b) Unpublished works; and (c) Adaptations. Autograph of Julian Marshall. (RM.19.f.9.)

These invaluable contributions to Handeliana are not generally known. It is true that much of the material in them has been recorded elsewhere in other forms, but they should be consulted by Handelians engaged in research, especially in conjunction with Schœlcher's Cambridge and Paris Catalogues, his life of Handel and Julian Marshall's Collection and Catalogue in the National Library of Scotland.

Handel. A Symposium, edited by Gerald Abraham, was published in 1954 (O.U.P.) and I contributed to it a *Catalogue of Handel's Works*. It was prepared under great personal stress during the last illness of my wife, and was done in a few weeks – fortunately I had the material scattered about in my library in one form or another. Those who may not have seen it may like to know that it gives the dates of production and publication of the works, with particulars of the location of the autographs and other important early manuscripts, with some bibliographical and other material.

The Catalogue which I contributed to *Grove's Dictionary of Music and Musicians*, fifth edition edited by Eric Blom, (vol. IV, pp. 50–60, 1954), was on different lines as laid down for me by the Editor. I would have preferred to include more details, but as it stands, this catalogue and the one in the "Symposium", supplement each other and present the Handelian with most of what he may want to know in approaching the study of any of the works for the first time.

An indispensable compilation that will eliminate the reading of a lot of other works is Dr. Otto Deutsch's *Handel. A Documentary Biography* (Adam & Charles Black, London, 1955). I met Dr. Deutsch in the early days of his stay in England just before the last war, and we contemplated doing some joint Handel and Walsh work together; but for various reasons this was not possible. Comprehensive and useful as the *Handel Documentary Biography* is, there are, as could be expected in so wide a subject, a number of omissions and errors. To a German edition of the work to be prepared in Halle, I have supplied much supplementary and corrective material, although I have a high regard for the *Documentary* as it stands. Deutsch was engaged in 1946 by the Committee of *The British Union – Catalogue of Early Music*, of which I was a founder member, to prepare and edit that work – which he did until 1950, when Edith B. Schnapper was appointed in his stead, the work being published in 1957 at £21 the two volumes (Butterworth's Scientific Publications, London).

The Handel section in *The British Union – Catalogue* gives a good overall picture of the locations of copies, although in many cases the identification of the editions is wrong – but even so I found it very useful when preparing my Handel Catalogue and writing innumerable letters to the various libraries where certain copies were reported to be.

I must mention Dr. Deutsch's kindness in presenting me with a typescript copy of the Schœlcher Catalogue which is in the

Mann Library, King's College, Cambridge. The possession of this has saved me much correspondence and probably many journeys to Cambridge. The catalogue is a valuable scource of detailed information about the works and the manuscripts, with invaluable notes by Dr. A. H. Mann, and can only be consulted outside King's College in the few copies of Deutsch's typescript which he sold or gave away, the title of which is, "*A Catalogue of The Works of G. F. Handel,* by Victor Schœlcher in collaboration with M. B. Lacy, translated by Miss S. A. A. P. Mann with notes by A. H. Mann. Edited, with a Preface and an Index by Otto Erich Deutsch, Cambridge, 1941. Copyright reserved."

The Fitzwilliam Museum, Cambridge, famous for its fine collection of miscellaneous art and historical treasures, includes besides, a collection of manuscript and printed music which gives it great importance among the chief musical libraries of Britain. Of particular interest to Handelians is the unique set of sketch-books and miscellaneous manuscripts in the handwriting of Handel. A "*Catalogue of the Music in the Fitzwilliam Museum, Cambridge,* by J. A. Fuller-Maitland, M.A., F.S.A., and A. H. Mann, Mus.D., Oxon", was issued in 1893 (Cambridge University Press, London). Dr. Mann was responsible for the arranging and cataloguing of the Handel manuscripts and sketches, which he did with great thoroughness giving detailed references to manuscripts and editions elsewhere. When it is pointed out that this section of the catalogue covers pp. 159–227 it will be realized how important the material is. It includes every branch of Handel's output, a number of variants and unpublished items, supplementary passages and alternative readings to existing copies of the works elsewhere. In addition the collection contains a number of Handel manuscripts not part of the sketch-books, and many Walsh and Randall printed editions. The scholarly notes by Dr. Mann, the general excellence of the catalogue as a whole, and the comprehensive index make the work of the Handelian who wishes to use the collection an easy matter.

7

Handel's Dramatic Oratorios and Masques, by Winton Dean (O.U.P., London, 1959) is a comprehensive and valuable work of original research, packed full of historical, bibliographical, musical and technical knowledge. It will remain a standard authority for the future. Written in a witty, engaging, and a highly critical way, but with sound knowledge and scholarship behind it, it has, however, the grave demerit of trying to prove that Handel's music is that of a humanist and has no especial Christian significance. He refers to *Messiah* as "untouched by mystical feeling, and inspired more by ethical humanism than by the doctrine of any Church" (p. 38), and goes on to say later, "there is a case for considering *L'Allegro* the more strictly religious work of the two" (*Messiah* and *L'Allegro*, p. 320).

On p. 325 he writes:

> "The dramatic inspiration of the style blows away the contention that the mainspring of *Messiah* was moral improvement. At the same time it supplies the leaven without which this peculiar masterpiece might never have expanded from a heavy and indigestible lump, and would assuredly not have ridden so buoyantly down the centuries".

An odd quotation or two is to be hardly just to Dean's work, but the point I wish to make is that scholars and writers who, looking at the eighteenth-century Handel and the interpretation of him in the nineteenth and the early years of the twentieth century and who feel that the composer has been unduly weighted with Protestant evangelism, are not fair to the subject when the Handel they create for us is a present day figure fashioned out of their own philosophy.

This imposing book deserves more attention than can be given to it here, and however much we may disagree with some of Dean's conclusions and interpretations, his arresting and illuminating comments are well worth serious consideration – as is much of what he has written elsewhere, especially about the operas. I am deeply grateful to the author for a complimentary copy of his book.

Dr. Percy M. Young has written on so many musical subjects that it is hardly sufficient to call him a Handelian, although I have known him personally best in that capacity, especially at the Halle Handel Festivals from time to time. Though not so ambitious a work as Winton Dean's, Young's *The Oratorios of Handel* (Dennis Dobson, London, 1949) is an important contribution to the subject, containing lots of suggestive ideas – some rather fanciful – but written in a very individual and penetrating style.

His *Handel* (Master Musicians, J. M. Dent & Sons, London, 1947) is one of the most informative of modern biographies, packed full of facts and ideas. Percy Young was the other English guest besides myself to be honoured with the Handel Prize in Halle in 1961. (*See* also pp. 88, 89.)

Of specialist contributors to Handelian literature reference must be made to Doctor Frederick Hudson of Newcastle-on-Tyne, who I met at the Handel Festival at Halle in 1959. He is editing for the Hallische Händel Ausgabe the Concerti Grossi, Op. 3, and found it necessary to study the watermarks used in Walsh's and copyists' paper – a subject also dealt with by Professor Larsen.[1] At the Festival in 1959 Doctor Hudson read a learned and comprehensive paper on this subject: 'Wasserzeichen in Händelschen Manuskripten und Drucken.' This was published, with facsimiles of the watermarks, in *Händel-Ehrung der Deutschen Demokratischen Republik* . . . 1959. *Konferenzbericht*, pp. 193–206. (Deutscher Verlag für Musik, Leipzig, 1961.)

With reference to the Concertos I cannot accept Doctor Hudson's and Professor H. F. Redlich's claim to have found a new Handel Concerto in one of the Walsh editions of Op. 3.[2]

The British Museum staged a *Messiah* Exhibition, from May to July 1951, in co-operation with the London Choral Society, and with the support of the Arts Council of Great Britain. It

[1] See pp. 87, 88.
[2] H. F. Redlich: A new "Oboe Concerto" by Handel. (*Musical Times*, August 1956, pp. 409–410); Smith: *Handel. A Descriptive Catalogue*, pp. 218–19.

included items from sources other than the Museum – among which was the only known copy of the First Edition of the *Songs in Messiah*, which I lent from my collection.[1] An interesting catalogue was issued, and is still obtainable at the Museum.

A Purcell-Handel Festival was held in London, June 1959, presented by The Arts Council of Great Britain, The British Council, The British Museum, The British Broadcasting Corporation and The London County Council. This was indeed a large scale tribute to the two composers and included a Commemorative Exhibition at The British Museum from May to August. The official catalogue of the Exhibition, containing 246 items and a number of illustrations is a very interesting and informative publication.

The "Purcell-Handel Festival. London, June 1959", the official Book listing all the events of the Festival and containing a number of important articles and illustrations is a clear proof of how Handel has at last come into his own as someone with a claim to being more than the composer of *Messiah* and one or two other works but otherwise of little interest to the British people. Among the interesting details in the Festival Book is the listing of sixty-seven provincial towns where commemorative celebrations and performances occurred, besides the many events that took place in London, and the following articles:

"Handel in England", Julian Herbage.
"Handel's Dramatic Works", Winton Dean.
"Handel and the English Church", Basil Lam.
"Handel's Instrumental Music", Hans F. Redlich.
"Purcell and Handel: A Comparison", J. A. Westrup.
"The Royal Society of Musicians", J. H. C.
"Handel in Mayfair", Gwen Ferguson.

[1] A copy from the same plates, but with MS. additions, is in the Schœlcher Collection, Paris.

16

HANDEL'S OPERAS AND STAGE PERFORMANCES OF THE ORATORIOS IN ENGLAND 1925–64

THE MODERN REVIVAL of Handelian opera in England got off to a slow start, and something has been said about some occasional performances of operas and stage productions of oratorios. An attempt is now made here to list other major productions by various enthusiastic conductors, producers, the B.B.C., and societies that have contributed to the now firmly-established place of Handel as an opera composer whose works are finding increasing support in this country. Brought together in this way one is surprised at the amount that has been done and is likely to be forgotten by or unknown to Handelians unless made generally more readily accessible to them. This list of miscellaneous productions which may have omitted some important events is followed by an account of the work of the Handel Opera Society and of Frances and Alan Kitching.

One of the earliest of modern stage productions of the oratorios was that of *Semele* at the New Theatre, Cambridge, February 10–14, 1925. The work, staged for the first time, was produced by Denis Arundell, with designs by Douglas Williams. The music was prepared by Dr. Cyril B. Rootham, who conducted, the performers being local amateurs, except for some of the orchestra and Bertha Steventon (Semele) and John Dean (Jupiter). Barclay Squire published an informative article on the work in *The Musical Times*, February 1925, and Percy Scholes gave an interesting report on the performacne in the March number of the same journal.

The first of the present-day Societies to put Handel's oratorios on the English stage was apparently the Falmouth Opera Singers, an amateur opera company founded in 1923 by the Misses Maisie and Evelyn Radford, and which came into being with a performance of Gluck's *Orpheus* and is still very much alive to-day. Since then performances of works by Mozart, Purcell, Pergolesi and others have been regularly given; but of special significance for Handelians were the following oratorios as stage productions:

Samson. Polytechnic Hall, Falmouth, October 23, 24, 25, 1929. Edith Blight, F.R.C.O., conductor. M. and E. Radford, producers. Geoffrey Dunn (Samson), Dorothy Shipman (Dalila), Percy Cowell (Harapha). *The Times*, October 28, 1929 contained a long and eulogistic report of this production, probably the first of *Samson* on the English stage.

Saul. Princess Pavilion, Falmouth, November 18, 19, 20, 1931. Edith Blight, conductor. M. and E. Radford, producers. Percy Cowell (Saul), Louis Tregunna (David), Muriel Peters (Merab). Reported in *The Times*, November 19, and *The Western Morning News*, November 20, 1931.

Athalia. Princess Pavilion, Falmouth, November 25, 26, 27, 1935. M. Radford, conductor. M. and E. Radford, producers. Assisted by Phyllis Carey-Foster (Athalia) and the St. Mawes Choral Society. Muriel Peters (Josabeth), Percy Cowell (Abner), Louis Tregunna (Joad).

Acis and Galatea. Princess Pavilion, Falmouth, June 25, 26, 1941. M. Radford, conductor. M. and E. Radford, producers. Muriel Peters (Galatea), Eric Starling (Acis), George Parker (Polyphemus).

Perseus and Andromeda. Princess Pavilion, Falmouth, June 30, July 1, 1943. M. Radford, conductor. M. and E. Radford, producers. George Parker (Cepheus), Muriel Peters (Andromeda). This work was the almost forgotten "Jupiter in Argos" with a new libretto by Albert W. Latham, formerly broadcast by the B.B.C., October 8, 1935, as recorded earlier (p. 57).

Belshazzar. Princess Pavilion, Falmouth, June 19, 20, 21, 1946.

M. Radford, conductor. M. and E. Radford, producers. Geoffrey Dunn (Belshazzar), George Parker (Daniel).

Samson. Polytechnic Hall, Falmouth, July 9, 10, 11, 1958. M. Radford, conductor. M. and E. Radford, producers. David Galliver (Samson), Muriel Peters (Dalila), Roger Stalman (Harapha).

Acis and Galatea. Polytechnic Hall, Falmouth, July 26, 27, 28, 1961. M. Radford, conductor. M. and E. Radford, producers. Anne Keynes (Galatea), David Galliver (Acis), Kenwyn Barton (Polyphemus).

This enterprising society of which the soloists, chorus and orchestra are mainly amateurs deserves special notice as a pioneer of stage productions of Handel's oratorios. An interesting account of its work appeared as a pamphlet *The Falmouth Opera Singers, 1923 to 1946*, by D. C. Hare and E. H. Lepper.

The Cambridge University Musical Society gave stage performances of some of the oratorios from 1932 onwards, mostly under the conductorship of Cyril B. Rootham, and the Society organised a successful Handel Festival in 1935, referred to earlier (p. 57). The major works produced were as follows:

Samson. Cambridge, Guildhall. February 27, 28, 29, 1932. Cyril B. Rootham conductor. Camille Prior producer. (*Musical Times*, April, 1932, p. 363.)

Jephtha. Cambridge, Guildhall, February 16, 17, 18, 19, 20, 1934. Cyril B. Rootham conductor. Camille Prior producer. Gwendolen Raverat costumes and scenery. (*Musical Times*, February, 1934, p. 123; March, 1934, p. 270.)

The Choice of Hercules. Cambridge, King's College. June 11, 12, 13, 15, 1935. Open Air performance. Music under the direction of Bernhard Ord and Hubert Middleton. Camille Prior producer. Gwendolen Raverat and Elisabeth Vellacott costumes and setting.

Susanna. Given with *The Choice of Hercules* as above. June 11, 12, 13, 15, 1935. *Susanna*, November 16–20, 1937.

Saul. Cambridge, Guildhall. February 16–20, 1937. Six performances. Bernhard Ord conductor. Camille Prior producer. (*Musical Times*, March, 1937, p. 270.)

Solomon. Cambridge, Guildhall. February 3–7, 1948. Seven

performances. Boris Ord conductor. Camille Prior and Kurt Jooss producers. Choreography by Kurt Jooss. (*Musical Times*, April, 1948, p. 124.)

MISCELLANEOUS PERFORMANCES

(Some entries as indicated are taken from Winton Dean's *Handel's Dramatic Oratorios and Masques*, pp. 662–4.)

Theodora. Alton, Hants. May 11, 1927. Alton Choral Society. Susan Lushington conductor. Mrs. Thornley Gibson (Theodora), Thornley Gibson (Didymas), Nora Selby (Irene), Mr. Bohanna (Valens). (Dean.)

Julius Cæsar. Scala Theatre, London, by the London Opera Festival Company. Robert Stuart director. Announced for January 6, 8, 10, 13, 15, 1930 as part of the Festival December 30, 1929 – January 18, 1930, which was to include works by Mozart, Glück, Weber, Monteverdi, etc. The season was a financial failure and collapsed after a few performances including three of *Julius Cæsar*. This work was given in English, the translation of Haym's text by Robert Stuart, the music specially arranged by Gervase Hughes who in spite of modifications and considerable shortening of the opera, "endeavoured to preserve the spirit of the eighteenth century," with an orchestra "identical with that used in the first performance". The producer was Norman Marshall.

Rinaldo. Century Theatre, Archer Street, London, February, 1933. "Venture" Fellowship Centre, Notting Hill, February 24, 1933. Production by Miss Olive Daunt, probably the first modern stage revival of this opera in England. The work was abridged, adapted for performance, translated and conducted by Miss Daunt, B.A., A.R.C.M., who was music mistress of the Hammersmith Day Continuation School, pupils of which provided the cast and the orchestra. I was particularly pleased to have learned of this interesting experiment from Geoffrey Dunn and to have had particulars supplied by Miss Daunt, who is now Principal of the Durham Academy of Singing where, as she says, her policy is "to win the villagers to orthodox opera and music drama", her best artists coming "from the miners, as the pit world underground is so romantic it breeds imagination and the men are real and have no bogus pretentions". Of the Century Theatre performance Ferruccio Bonavia in *The Musical Times*, March, 1933, p. 270,

said, "A capital production ... Undeterred by the great difficulties which stood in her way ... Miss Daunt kept steadily to
her task of preparation and finally succeeded in a most creditable
effort". Stanley Verde said in *The Music Lover*, "The whole
thing glowed with art and courage ... All credit to Olive Daunt,
an excellent conductor, to May Burrell the producer, and to
Kathleen Tacchi, the dancing mistress". Of the "Venture"
performance Richard Capell wrote in *The Daily Telegraph*,
February 25, 1933, "The curious experience was to be had last
night ... of hearing Handel's first London Opera, *Rinaldo* performed by a company of London schoolgirls ... The singing,
while naturally immature, was never forced, and the result, if
not exactly Handelian, was musical ... *Rinaldo* contains admirable
music and the young girls whom Miss Daunt has trained will have
received a lesson in musical style to last them their lives."

Miss Daunt also staged other works than Handel's including
Lulli's *Amadis*, but for Handelians it is essential to remember her
Rinaldo, a pioneer effort to bring this magnificent and historic
work back to the stage where it is now firmly established as a full
scale opera by the performances under Charles Farncombe of The
Handel Opera Society at Sadler's Wells and in East Germany, as
recorded later on.

Saul. Birkbeck College, London, March 9, 10, 11, 1933. A stage
production by Geoffrey Dunn, a Handelian singer who had
appeared as Samson and Belshazzar in the Falmouth productions.
Also March 12, 1936. (Dean.)

Serse (*Xerxes*). Pollards Opera Festival, Loughton, Essex, June 15
(twice), September 13, 14, 1935. R.A.M., November 1935 (twice).
Translated and produced by Geoffrey Dunn, who also made
the translation of *Admetus*, *Giulio Cesare* (Act I) and of *Apollo and
Daphne* used in the B.B.C. broadcast performances. Dunn's
translation of *Xerxes* has been used in eleven stage performances
of the complete work. He also contributed the narrations broadcast before the B.B.C. performances of some of Handel's operas
or parts of them, and appeared as The First Elder in the Cambridge
production of *Susanna*, November 16, 1937.

Samson. Bryanston School, Dorset, December, 7 1936. Two
performances. Paul Rogers conductor. (Dean.)

Susanna. Cambridge, Arts Theatre, November 16–20. 1937. Six
performances. Boris Ord conductor. Camille Prior producer.

A small contingent of the C.U.M.S. assisted. (*Musical Times*, December, 1937, p. 1072.)

Belshazzar. London, Scala Theatre, May 16, 1938. One week. Workers Music Association. Warwick Braithwaite, John Allen. (Dean.) Referred to more fully on p. 141. Jennens's text adapted by Randall Swingler. The performance was under the artistic direction of Alan Bush, and the Boyd Neel String Orchestra supplemented with wood-wind, brass and an electrically amplified harpsichord, co-operated under the direction of Warwick Braithwaite. (*Musical Times*, June, 1938, p. 465.)

Belshazzar. London, Albert Hall, April 1939. The Festival of Music for the People. Jennens text adapted by Randall Swingler. Alan Bush conductor. (For *Daily Telegraph* report, April 8, 1939 see pp. 141-2.)

Samson. Aberdare, Coliseum, February 14, 1949. Six performances. Trecynon and District Choral Union. Sam Watts conductor. (Dean.)

Belshazzar. Cranleigh School, March 6, 1951. Two performances. Robin Wood conductor. Warren Green producer. (Dean.)

Jephtha. Aberdare, Coliseum, April 9, 1951. Six performances. Trecynon and District Choral Union. Sam Watts conductor. (Dean.)

Saul. Aberdare, Coliseum, May 24, 1952. Seven performances. Trecynon and District Choral Union. Sam Watts conductor. (Dean.)

Joshua. Aberdare, Coliseum, April 18, 1953. Seven performances. Trecynon and District Choral Union. Sam Watts conductor. David Franklin producer. (Dean.)

Athalia. Girton College, Cambridge. A delightful stage production by the Girton College Musical Society. March 5 and 6, 1954, which Dr. Hall and I attended. The conductor, a young woman, Ann Eminton, was most convincing. She got everything she could out of the company and the orchestra, in spite of the limitations of stage and setting. It was a successful, courageous effort, and Dr. Hall obtained a good recording of it.

Belshazzar. Aberdare, Coliseum, March 27, 1954. Seven performances. Trecynon and District Choral Union. Sam Watts conductor. David Franklin producer. (Dean.)

Acis and Galatea. Audley End House, May 1954. Two performances. George Barker conductor. (Dean.)

Saul. Bryanston School, Dorset. Open Air Theatre, June 10, 1954. Two performances. Paul Rogers conductor. (Dean.)

Semele. London, Chanticleer Theatre, December 13, 1954. Three performances. Opera in miniature. Robert Ponsonby conductor. Jack Phipps producer. (Dean.)

Samson. Leeds, Grand Theatre, October 14, 1958. Six performances. Covent Garden Opera Company. Raymond Leppard conductor. Herbert Graf producer. (Dean.) This production was also given at Covent Garden, November 24 and December 2, 12, 20, 1958 under Raymond Leppard. Herbert Graf producer. I took Dr. Dorothea Siegmund-Schultze, of Halle (whose husband, Professor Dr. Walther Siegmund-Schultze is the enthusiastic organizing secretary of the Handel Society there) to see this production.

Serse. Barber Institute of Fine Arts, Birmingham, March 4, 5, 1959. In English, translation by Geoffrey Dunn. Anthony Lewis conductor. Brian Trowell producer.

Alcina. Covent Garden by the Royal Swedish Opera, September 5, 9, 1960. Lars af Malmborg conductor.

Imeneo. Barber Institute of Fine Arts, Birmingham, March 23, 24, 1961. In English, translation by Nigel Fortune and Brian Trowell. Anthony Lewis conductor. Brian Trowell producer.

Alcina. Covent Garden. Franco Zeffirelli's production as a Masque and Ballet, March 8, 1962. Conductor Bryan Balkwill.

Tamerlane. Barber Institute of Fine Arts, Birmingham, March 21, 22, 1962. In English, translation by Nigel Fortune and Brian Trowell. Anthony Lewis conductor. Brian Trowell producer.

Ariodante. Barber Institute of Fine Arts, Birmingham, May 7, 9, 1964. In English, translation by Brian Trowell. Anthony Lewis conductor. Brian Trowell producer.

B.B.C. PERFORMANCES

Admeto. February 1, 2, 1947. In English, translation by Geoffrey Dunn. Stanford Robinson conductor.

Agrippina. January 1, 1954. In Italian. Recording of a Milan performance.

Alcina. Abridged version. March 22, 1959. Handel Opera Society. In English, translation by Charles Farncombe, conductor.

Ariodante. April 4, 1964. In Italian. Arnold Goldsbrough conductor.

Deidamia. February 11, 1962, January 6, 1963. In Italian. Arnold Goldsbrough conductor.

Giulio Cesare. Act. I. December 19, 1948, January 14, 1949. In English, translation by Geoffrey Dunn. Anthony Lewis conductor. September 17, 1951. In German. Recording of a Hamburg performance.

Hercules. July 12, 1960, Handel Opera Society. Charles Farncombe conductor.

Lotario. Act I. December 12, 1948. January 19, 1949. In Italian. Arnold Goldsbrough conductor.

Orlando. Act II. December 1, 1948, January 5, 1949. February 24, 1963, complete. In Italian. Arnold Goldsbrough conductor.

Rinaldo. February 25, 1948. In Italian. Recording of a Radio Italiana, Rome, performance. Conducted by Fernando Previtali.

Sosarme. Act II. December 6, 1948, February 7, 1949. January 31, February 1, 1955, complete. In Italian. Anthony Lewis conductor.

Xerxes. January 23, 25, 1948, January 28, 30, 1949. In English, translation by Geoffrey Dunn. Stanford Robinson conductor.

It was a fortunate day for Handel opera enthusiasts when "The Handel Opera Society" was established in London in 1955 under the patronage of the Earl of Harewood, with Professor Anthony Lewis as Chairman, and Charles Farncombe as Conductor. The St. Pancras Borough Council was interested in the scheme, and invited the Group to produce the first opera in the St. Pancras Assembly Rooms, St. Pancras Town Hall. There, on June 3, with all the limitations of the place – absence of staging facilities – and no previous experience as a Society, the opera *Deidamia* was given. It caught on. It was something new to many people, and the Society was greatly encouraged. Since then it has achieved increasing success and wide support, so that the performances nowadays, given at Sadler's Wells Theatre, are usually well booked up in advance – and Handel Opera has come to stay. Following is a list of the productions up to date – some having been given more than once; and *Rinaldo* having achieved the distinction of being given by the Society in East Berlin and at the Halle Handel Festival in 1961, where it was most enthusiastically received, as described below:

Deidamia. June 3, 1955. St. Pancras Town Hall.

Concert of Handel's Italian Church Music. November 27, 1955. Arts Council, St. James's Square.

Hercules. May 2, 1956. St. Pancras Town Hall.

Alcina. March 19, 20, 1957. St. Pancras Town Hall.

Theodora. February 25, 27, 28, 1958. St. Pancras Town Hall.

Solomon. May 7, 1958. St. James's Church, Piccadilly.

Alcina. Abridged version. March 22, 1959. B.B.C.

Rodelinda. June 24, 26, 1959. Sadler's Wells.

Semele. June 23, 25, 27, 1959. Sadler's Wells.

Concert, Handel, Bach, Haydn, February 28, March 26, 1960. St. Pancras Town Hall.

Radamisto. July 6, 7, 9, 1960. Sadler's Wells.

Hercules. July 5, 8, 1960. Sadler's Wells.

Hercules. Concert performance. July 12, 1960. Goldsmiths' Hall. Broadcast by B.B.C.

Three Musical Morality Plays by Carissimi. March 11, 1961. St. Pancras Town Hall.

Semele. May 16, 18, 1961. Sadler's Wells.

Rinaldo. May 17, 19, 20, 1961. Sadler's Wells.

Artaxerxes. T. A. Arne. March 14, 16, 1962. St. Pancras Town Hall.

Radamisto. July 18, 20, 1962. Sadler's Wells.

Jephtha. July 17, 19, 21, 1962. Sadler's Wells.

Carols for everyone. Concert. December 19, 1962. St. Pancras Town Hall.

Ulysses. John Christopher Smith. March, 12, 14, 1963. St. Pancras Town Hall.

Xerxes. June 19, 21, 24, 28, 1963. Sadler's Wells. Anthony Lewis conductor.

Giulio Cesare. June 20, 22, 26, 1963. Sadler's Wells. June 26 was a Gala Performance, with Joan Sutherland, for the Sunshine Homes for the Blind.

Jephtha. June 25, 27, 29, 1963. Sadler's Wells.

Acis and Galatea. December 1, 1963. Aberystwyth.

Carols for all. Concert. December 17, 1963. St. Pancras Town Hall.

L'Infedeltà Delusa. Haydn. March 18, 19, 1964. St. Pancras Town Hall.

Semele. July 7, 9, 1964. Sadler's Wells.

Richard I. July 8, 10, 11, 1964. Sadler's Wells.
Susanna. October 21, 1964. St. James's Church, Piccadilly.
Carols for Everyone. Concert, December 17, 1964. St. Pancras Town Hall.

This is a formidable achievement from scratch and one of the pleasing features about it is that Charles Farncombe is now quite rightly recognized as a scholarly musician and conductor of extreme sensibility and musical perception, who is also appreciated for his performances on the Continent and in the United States of America as well as here. As one of the early members of the Handel Opera Society it has been my pleasure to attend most of the performances, and to know that not only in East Germany or at Göttingen in West Germany can I see Handel operas convincingly produced. No Handelian in England should hesitate to join the Society and support its future work.

The following extracts from press reports, translated by Myrtle Muskett, show how the experienced audiences in East Germany received the Handel Opera Society's performances.

"The participation of the London Handel Opera Society will unquestionably be one of the high spots of the tenth Handel Festival in Halle. This optimistic forecast can be made because of the success, which can only be called triumphant, which the English visitors achieved when they gave two performances in the Berlin Komische Oper of their Festival contribution *Rinaldo*.

"Applause broke out a number of times during the actual performance, and at the end the London artists were kept on stage or called before the curtain for a quarter of an hour in order to receive the thanks of the excited audience." *National Zeitung*, Berlin, June 20, 1961.

"Handel's *Rinaldo* music, which counts among its most popular pieces the moving saraband, simple as a folksong, sung by the weeping, imprisoned Almirena, has such an abundance of melody, beauty and variety that it has lost none of its freshness and mastery. Charles Farncombe, the orchestral director, conducted with a fine feeling for its vocal line and its colourful orchestration ... The singing was in general very artistic, with a tasteful understanding of expression and style ... With its baroque, aesthetically beautiful presentation of *Rinaldo* it has stimulated comparison with other interpretations, which for their part should also stimulate the English visitors, who have so rightly been given such a warm reception." *Berliner Zeitung*, June 21, 1961.

"For the first time an English ensemble is visiting Halle for the Handel Festival. Their production of the magic opera, *Rinaldo*, which Handel first wrote for London in 1711, was for us an event of a very special kind, so to speak a piece of opera history brought to life. Uniform in its portrayal, musically beautiful and nobly executed (conductor Charles Farncombe), it struck admiration from the audience who showed their gratitude to the orchestra, the producer and the conductor with heartfelt applause." *BZ am Abend*, Berlin, June 23, 1961.

"A significant event of this year's tenth Handel Festival was last Wednesday's guest performance by the London Handel Opera Society of Handel's opera *Rinaldo*. It was a brilliant success; conductor, soloists, the whole ensemble were given a jubilant reception." (*Freiheit*, Halle, June 24, 1961.)

See Handel and *Rinaldo*. Charles Farncombe. (*Opera*, Vol. 12, No. 5, May 1961, pp. 305–7.)

Händels Oper *Rinaldo*. Charles Farncombe. (Programme of Halle performance, 1961, pp. 5–7.)

Hercules was staged as an opera on March 31 and April 1, 1939, by Frances Rowe (now Kitching) conductor, and Alan Kitching, producer, under the auspices of The Opera Club, Merstham. This "almost entirely amateur production", the costumes and properties of which were designed and made by the conductor and producer, "attempted to preserve something of the eighteenth century tradition both on the stage and in the orchestra".

The later productions of Handel operas by Frances and Alan Kitching at the Unicorn Theatre, Abingdon, Berkshire, deserve special emphasis. There, with the support of the Arts Council and the Abingdon Borough Council these two enthusiasts and the Unicorn Theatre Club have brought Handel to the stage in a most fascinating way. In a small, intimate theatre holding a handful of people, with the musicians gallery above the tiny stage with its eighteenth-century settings and atmosphere, one feels almost part of the performance. Frances Kitching, who is responsible for the musical arrangements, directs with great skill and effectiveness, and is ably supported by the delightful productions of her husband, who is also responsible for the translation of the libretti. The whole undertaking is a unique and highly commendable tribute to the effectiveness of Handel on the stage to-day when essayed by producers with the technical knowledge, ability and zeal of Frances and Alan Kitching, so ably supported by all those who have contributed to the success of the productions:

Orlando. May 6, 7, 8, 9, 1959.
Saul. May 14, 1959 (at the Corn Exchange).
Hercules. June 30, July 1, 2, 5, 6, 1960.
Parthenope. May 4, 5, 6, 8, 9, 1961.
Floridante. May 10, 11, 12, 14, 15, 16, 1962.
Giustino. February 15, 16, 1963. A shortened version by the girls of Our Lady's Convent, Abingdon.
Agrippina. June 27, 28, 29, July 1, 2, 3, 1963.
Admetus. May 7, 8, 9, 11, 13, 1964.

Annals of Opera 1597–1940. Compiled from the Original Sources by Alfred Loewenberg (W. Heffer & Sons, Limited, Cambridge, 1943) is such a monumental classic that it may appear superfluous to mention it. But it is so essential as a record of works, performances, librettists, etc., that no Handelian can afford to be without it. I make mention of it, first of all because of its value as a source book, and secondly because I knew the author well. A great scholar, an indefatigable worker, one who was always ready to help me in any way, a refugee who suffered great loss under the Nazi régime, but never appeared embittered or frustrated. He continued his musical and other research work in the British Museum until his premature death, probably due to overwork, December 29, 1949.

An invaluable work for any producer or student of Handel opera is Hellmuth Christian Wolff's *Die Händel-Oper auf der modernen Bühne. Ein Beitrag zu Geschichte und Praxis der Opern-Bearbeitung und -Inszenierung in der Zeit von 1920 bis 1965.* (Deutscher Verlag für Musik, Leipzig, 1957.) Not only does this attractive volume tell the story of the renaissance of Handel opera in Germany in modern times, but it includes ninety-nine fine illustrations of stage scenes of operas over the period, with comments on them, problems of performance and other interesting details.

17

CHORAL PERFORMANCES OF
ORATORIOS – HUBERT LANGLEY –
BERNARD ROSE – ANTHONY BERNARD –
HELMUT KOCH

THE ORATORIOS OF Handel have not suffered over the years the
same eclipse as the operas, although *Messiah* has been the most
frequently presented work, and some of the others are hardly
known. It is unnecessary to record here the many performances
that have been given by the B.B.C. and others up and down the
country, but attention must be drawn to some, especially to the
work of one enthusiast, Hubert Langley, who has persistently
given performances of Handel's works other than *Messiah*.

The Foundling Hospital, of which Handel was a Governor
and where he performed *Messiah* for the benefit of the institution
was sold in 1926 and pulled down, and the work is now carried
on at Berkamsted in new buildings opened in 1935. In the fine
offices of the administration, built near the old site, are the portraits
and paintings, and many other interesting possessions of the Hospital, including the Godfrey Kneller portrait and Roubiliac bust
of Handel; a manuscript score and parts of *Messiah* and other
relics. From time to time performances of the oratorios are given
here under the direction of Hubert Langley, one of the Governors.
They are very individual interpretations, prepared with great
care and performed by chorus and orchestra, largely friends of the
conductor, and the best professional and amateur soloists obtainable. I have always enjoyed these friendly and sociable occasions
The handsome gallery where the performances take place is just
the right setting for Handel, with a small orchestra and chorus

The works I have heard over the years from 1950 onwards are: Hercules, Belshazzar, Samson, Deborah, Joshua, Judas Maccabæus, Esther, Saul and Jephtha – largely the tribute of one enthusiastic Handelian to the master whose work he admires, understands and produces as faithfully as he can.

Dr. Bernard Rose, Fellow, Instructor in Music and Organist of Magdalen College, Oxford, has made his contribution to Handel performances in that City as follows:

Three Coronation Anthems.	June 1940.
Alexander's Feast.	November 1947.
Jephtha.	March 1952.
Susanna.	March 1953.
Sixth Chandos Anthem.	November 1954.
Theodora.	June 1955.

(All with the Eglesfield Musical Society, Chorus and Orchestra, Oxford, in the Hall of Queen's College.)
Concerti Grossi, Op. 6, Nos. 5, 6, 7, 12 (1961 and 1962). (With the Handel String Orchestra, Oxford, in the Holywell Music Room.)

Dr. Rose is editing Handel's *Susanna* for publication in the Hallische Händel Ausgabe, and has been a guest at the Halle Handel Festivals, 1957, etc. I have frequently had the pleasure of staying with him and his family, and enjoying the services at Magdalen College, where the music is always of a very high standard. He is an erudite and dedicated musician who is satisfied with nothing but the best. I very much treasure the friendship of Bernard and his wife who have been extremely kind to me.

Mention must be made of two little known works – *The Choice of Hercules* (not to be confused with the oratorio, *Hercules*); and *Joseph and his Brethren*, both edited by Norman Stone. The former was issued in 1954 (Novello & Co.) and the latter awaits publication.

The Choice of Hercules, which runs for about 50 minutes, was broadcast by the B.B.C. on June 15, 17, 1953 under the direction of the late Anthony Bernard – a sparkling and brilliant performance of this delightful "Musical Interlude" (as Handel called it). I was present at the first broadcast and count it as one of the most entrancing experiences of Handel unknown to me.

Joseph and his Brethren was broadcast on January 17, 1959 under the same conductor, Anthony Bernard, with his London Chamber Singers, and a strong team of soloists. The libretto, a copy of which is in the British Museum, is by the Rev. James Miller. It is very uneven in quality and descends in places to mawkish sentimentality in the worst style of eighteenth-century drama, and it was so lengthy that Handel cut it considerably before setting it, and even then the work takes over three hours to perform. Some of the recitatives, and words of one or two of the arias are so ridiculous that Norman Stone found it necessary to alter the libretto to something less risible in order that Handel's glorious music should not suffer by it, and in at least one case an aria had to be omitted from the performance because the words were so impossible. Having said this it remains to say that Handel's music rises supreme above all obstacles and the oratorio contains many moments of serene beauty and enchantment; dramatic intensity as the story unfolds, and concluding with the interpolated final chorus of the Dettingen Anthem, "The King shall rejoice". It is to be hoped that Norman Stone's version will be published. Three other performances of a Handel work edited by Stone which were broadcast by the B.B.C. were those of *L'Allegro ed il Penseroso* which took place on October 1 and 2, 1950 with the late ever-lamented Constant Lambert as conductor, under whose baton a scintillating and thrilling performance of the work will long be remembered by all who listened to it. A repeat performance was given on May 25, 1951, at the Goldsmiths' Hall under the auspices of The City Music Club, with Clarence Raybould as conductor.

As a singer known better to an earlier generation as soloist and ensemble singer, Norman Stone spent eight years as tenor in The English Singers, a sextet of madrigal singers (see *Grove's Dictionary*, fifth edition, vol. II, pp. 51–2, 1954), who toured the Continent of Europe, America, and Canada and finished up with a world tour. On the dissolution of the partnership of the six solo singers (singing in ensemble as a single unit with the same personnel throughout those years) Stone formed a Quartet of the same name, and during the war years 1939–45 gave concerts throughout England, Scotland and Wales under the aegis of C.E.M.A. (Council for the Encouragement of Music and the Arts) – later to become The Arts Council. He has composed and published many part-songs and arrangements of traditional airs, folksongs and other music for ensemble singing. After the end of the late war he turned his attention to editorship, being commissioned by the B.B.C. soon after the formation of the Third Programme, to edit various works by composers of the pre-Bach period, from Schütz and his contemporaries through the centuries to their culmination and consummation in the works of Bach and Handel – since when he has become an enthusiastic Handelian research student and editor. Norman and I are great friends and collaborators, and have visited the Handel Festivals in Halle together.

In addition to *The Choice of Hercules* and *Joseph and his Brethren* mentioned above, Anthony Bernard conducted performances of other Handel works, as follows:

Concert at the Foundling Hospital, June 23, repeated June 24, 25, 1927 – the last before the old building was demolished. The programme included the *Fireworks* and *Water Music*, two arias from the Foundling Hospital Anthem ("Blessed are they that consider the poor") and scenes from *Julius Cæsar* in costume.
Jephtha. Concert performance. B.B.C., March 15, 1955.
Chandos Anthem No. 8 ("O come let us sing unto the Lord"). B.B.C., January 6, 1959.
Gramophone recordings for the Club Français du Disque, Paris:

Ode for St. Cecilia's Day.
Organ Concertos, Op. 4, Nos. 1, 2 and 4.
Concerti Grossi, Op. 3, Nos. 2, 4 and 5.
Oboe Concerto in G minor.

Fireworks Music.
Water Music.

One event I was pleased to attend was the performance of *Belshazzar* by the Deutschland Radio Singers, the Berlin Radio Choir and the East Berlin Symphony Orchestra under Helmut Koch, at the Royal Festival Hall, London, on October 5, 1959, following a performance at Coventry. I had frequently heard this company in Halle, and was particularly interested that they should get through the barrier of international difficulties and perform here. Unfortunately for some reason or other the audience was very thin, but the critics were warm in their praises of the performance. No musical group or society, no prominent musicians showed the slightest public interest in the visit of the company, and their only reception was by Norman Stone and myself, who conducted some of the principals round London, into the City, to the Tower of London, on the river trip back to Westminster, and to the Abbey, where they were anxious to see the tomb of Handel their great master. I felt that the impression on the East Germans of English hospitality must have been very bad. The Choir and Orchestra under the conductorship of Rudolf Kleinert on October 4, 1959, performed Beethoven's *Missa Solemnis* at the Festival Hall.

18

INTERESTING HANDELIANA –
SOME LUCKY FINDS

ALTHOUGH IT IS hardly likely that important new facts about Handel's life will come to light, from time to time discoveries are made about the works themselves, and two or three examples from my own experience are interesting, and concern the oratorio *Esther*, the opera *Admetus* and the question of Handel's blindness, the Suites and the solo cantata *Venus and Adonis*.

In *Music and Letters*, April 1950, I told of the existence of a manuscript sold by Ellis of 29 New Bond Street some years earlier, which proved that the performances of *Esther*, February 23 and March 1 and 3, 1732, were all at the Crown and Anchor Tavern, in the Strand; the first not at Bernard Gates's house as usually stated. It is not necessary to repeat here details of the manuscript and reasons for my suggestion that Burney (who first gave the information as received from Dr. Randall and Thomas Barrow, who took part in the performance), was probably wrong about Gates's house. It was some years after I had written the article in *Music and Letters* that strange corroboration of my opinion came to hand. I had asked a young typist to type a short addition to an article of mine about performances of *Messiah* at the Crown and Anchor Tavern in 1744 and 1747. When she gave me the typed copy she said that she believed that her mother had some music with a reference to the Crown and Anchor on it. I was tremendously anxious to see it, which I was able to do. Imagine my surprise when I recognized that it was another manuscript score of *Esther* with all the same particulars in it (dates and places of performance, singers, the choirs taking part and the situation of the Chorus between the Stage and the Orchestra) as in the Ellis copy. I immediately offered to buy the manuscript, but the young lady's mother preferred to keep it. Two or three years afterwards the daughter wrote to say that her mother would be pleased now to sell the manuscript to me at the price I originally offered. To-day it is one of my most treasured Handel items, and I think there is every reason to think that it is the earliest form of the work as performed for the Duke of Chandos.

On March 12, 16, 19, 23, and April 6, 1754, *Admeto* was performed at the King's Theatre under the management of Francesco Vanneschi, with which Handel is said to have had no connection. *Collector's Luck* placed in my hands a few years ago a copy of the second issue of J. Cluer's score of the opera, which quite clearly proves that the 1754 production had some authority from Handel. The autograph of this opera is missing, except for trifling fragments. The copy of my score was clearly used by Handel in the preparation of the work for the 1754 revival. The composer has indicated in his characteristic pencil hand the changes in the order of the arias, the alterations of keys to suit the singers whose names are pencilled throughout the work. This is of immense importance as evidence of the fact that in spite of failing sight and operations on his eyes, Handel was not completely blind in 1754. I do not believe that he was for years without any sight, or even at the end of his life – a subject which I dealt with fully in a speech I made in Halle in 1959, on "Handel's life in England", published in German in *Händel-Ehrung der Deutschen Demokratischen Republik, Halle. 11–19 April 1959. Konferenzbericht*", pp. 73–79.

The editing of the Harpsichord Suites has always been a problem to those who wish to get behind the early Cluer and Walsh editions. There are, however, no autographs of these two volumes, although the King's Music Library now contains a number of "Pieces for the Harpsichord", purchased by Squire at the Aylesford sale, edited by Squire and J. A. Fuller-Maitland and published by Schott in 1928. The reasonable assumption is that the Cluer and Walsh volumes are only selected items from a larger number composed by Handel. The Cluer (Premier Volume) 1720 and successive issues, and the Walsh (Second Volume) c. 1733 are taken as authoritative issues, but again an unexpected find raises some questions. It is a copy of the Suites, Second Volume, title page as the accepted Walsh, but with the imprint blocked out. The music is from the same plates as the Walsh (No. 5 in *Handel. A Descriptive Catalogue*, etc.), but with the Suites in a different order commencing with the "Preludio" (Walsh, Vol. II, p. 64, Suite 9), after which follow Nos. 8, 3, 4, 5, 2, 6, 7, 1, 9 of the accepted Walsh. This order is not found again in the eighteenth century and early editions until Preston's c. 1810, of which I have a copy. The problem of order is further complicated by the existence of the Jeanne Roger work, *Pieces à un & Deux Clavecins Composées Par M*ʳ* Hendel*, published at Amsterdam c. 1721 or perhaps earlier, which consists of items from the Cluer and Walsh volumes differently grouped, and including three numbers not in either of those editions. An imperfect copy is in the Bodleian Library.[1] Arnold Goldsbrough was editing the Suites (Vol. II) for the Halle Handel Edition, but died unexpectedly in December 1964. He had a wide knowledge of Handel and had frequently edited and conducted works of the composer for the B.B.C. and elsewhere. As organist, conductor and teacher he could be relied upon to deal in a scholarly manner with the editorial problems that the Suites present. The Goldsbrough Orchestra, which he founded, has an established place in English music to-day, and his position and work as organist of St. Martin-in-the-Fields (1924–35) is remembered with very great pleasure by thousands. Arnold was a dear friend of mine, and to spend a few days with him and his wife at Lower Haresbrook, Tenbury Wells, Worcester, was an inspiration and a delightful experience.

Arnold Goldsbrough's performances of Handel's works for the B.B.C. included:

Aci, Galatea e Polifermo.	June 28, 1948.
Acis and Galatea.	February 1, 1962.
L'Allegro ed il Penseroso.	November 8, 1962
Aminta e Filleda, cantata.	April 4, 1948.

[1] Smith. *Handel. A Descriptive Catalogue*, etc., pp. 251–52.

Apollo e Dafne, cantata.	June 9, 1959.
Chandos Anthem, "Have mercy upon me, O God".	February 15, 1959.
Deidamia.	February 11, 1962, January 6, 1963.
Dixit Dominus.	September 18, 1961.
Jephtha.	May 11, 1950.
Ninfe e Pastori, cantata.	August, 4, 6, 1957.
Nisi Dominus.	March 19, 1957.
Orlando.	February 24, 1963.
Silete venti, motet	June 23, 1959, January 20, 1963.
Ariodante.	April 4, 1964.

Arnold Goldsbrough also conducted a performance of the *Caecilien Ode* (*Ode for St. Cecilia's Day*) at the Halle Handel Festival, June, 22 1955, with soloists, choir and orchestra of the Landestheater, Halle.

I bought from a dealer a small collection of Manuscripts of works by Handel and others. These on examination showed that they had originally belonged to the Aylesford family. One of the items has the signature of the young Lord Guernsey (afterwards the Earl of Aylesford) and another in a contemporary hand, the note, "N.B. from the Earl of Aylesford's Collection". The Handel items are:

> An unpublished Harpsichord Suite, presumably by Handel (see below).
> *Alessandro Severo*. Overture, four string parts.
> *Belshazzar*. Overture, four string parts.
> *Hercules*. Overture, four strings, hautbois I and II and cembalo parts.
> *Serse*. Overture, four string parts.
> Concerto Grosso in C. H-G 21, pp. 63–82. Seven parts, wanting Violino secondo concertino, viola and basso. (Performed in *Alexander's Feast*.)
> Concerto in D major. H-G 47, pp. 80–98. (Used in the *Fireworks Music*.) Hautboy primo and secondo, and organo parts.
> Miscellaneous items: Three numbers from *L'Allegro*; one from *Deborah*; the March from the *Ode for St. Cecilia's Day*; two numbers from G.B.Bononcini's *Astarto*; odd parts of Concertos by Richard Mudge and some unidentified items.

With regard to the "Suite", presumably by Handel, this is without Handel's name, as is the March from the *Ode for St. Cecilia's Day*, which precedes it in the same volume. It is followed by "Aire Diana and Endymion", (by Pescetti, unnamed). The "Suite" consists of six numbers (twelve movements), only the third number ("Sarabande") with title. The evidence that the work may be by Handel is based on the facts that the fifth number (Minuet in two movements), occurs in "Pieces Pour le Clavecin Composées par G. F. Handel Ve Ouvrage ... London. John What", etc. (*Handel. A Descriptive Catalogue*, p. 276); As "Minuet d'Handel" in "Recueil de Pieces ... Accomodé pour les Flûtes travers^s ... Par M. Blavet (Vol. I, pp. 62, 63, BM.b.33. *Handel. A Descriptive Catalogue*, p. 276), and also in an eighteenth-century manuscript of miscellaneous items in Gerald Coke's Collection, dated 1759 as "Menuet de Mr Handel'. The other numbers of the "Suite" have not been traced elsewhere.

One day while casually looking through *Poems on Several Occasions with Some Select Essays in Prose*, by John Hughes (1677–1720), author of one number in *Acis and Galatea* ("Would you gain the tender creature"), I came upon the text of *Venus and Adonis, a Cantata Set by Mr. Handel*. This was new to me and I endeavoured to find out something else about it, and whether Handel's music was known. Finally I ran to earth music and text of the two arias ("Dear Adonis" and "Transporting Joy"), of the cantata (without that of the two recitatives) in the Manuscript Department of the British Museum (Add. MSS. 31993, Nos. 23 and 24, ff. 46b etc.), where they occurred in a volume of miscellaneous opera songs, without any mention of composer. An examination of the music seemed to establish without doubt that they were by Handel. The interesting facts about them are fully given in the Introduction to the edition of the two numbers, edited by me, with music arranged by Havergal Brian (Augener Ltd., London, 1938). Unfortunately Brian's arrangement was too sophisticated with a complex continuo, for the edition to be generally accepted. Norman Stone and I have prepared another edition, supplying and adapting from *L'Allegro* and *Acis and*

Galatea music for the recitatives. The whole cantata was performed by Philine Fischer, the prima donna of the Halle Opera, at a Chamber Music Concert at the Halle Handel Festival on June 19, 1962. This edition will be published in due course by Deutscher Verlag für Musik, Leipzig.

In 1733 a pamphlet was published, no copy of which was said to be known, but fortunately one came into my hands a few years ago. The title page reads:

> "Do you know what you are about? Or a Protestant Alarm to Great Britain: Proving our late Theatric Squabble, a Type of the present Contest for the Crown of Poland; and that the Division between *Handel* and *Senesino*, has more in it than we imagine. Also That the latter is no Eunuch, but a Jesuit in Disguise; with other Particulars of the greatest Importance.
>
> "God save his Church, our King, and Realm,
> And send us Peace, and Trade, Amen.
> "London. Printed for J. Roberts, at the Oxford Arms in Warwick Lane. 1733. Price 6d."

This pamphlet, which mentions others besides Handel and Senesino, has also special reference to Signora Cuzzoni, named as "Catsoni, so call'd from *Catso*, a delicious Fruit which grows in several Parts of *Italy*, and of which this Lady is extremely fond, even to Voracity". Some of the reference and allusions are very suggestive. I will only quote the first part of the Preface:

> "I hereby exhort and admonish, nay entreat and conjure our Nobility, Gentry, and others, whom it may concern, That before they subscribe, or at least pay any of their Money to H--d-l, or S---n---o, they take especial Care to be satisfied, that the Singers are true Protestants, and well affected to the present Government. Those who are not so, to conform and take the Oaths: To encourage which Good Work, the Salaries of those who shall so conform, should be doubled. But above all things, let Care be taken that there be no Prevarication, Equivocation, Mental Reservation, no Jesuitical Quibbles, or other Papistical

Legerdemain; but that all be acted fair, square, and above-board:
This done, let it be particularly covenanted, that they sing not in
an unknown Tongue, which is contrary to the Statute made and
provided for that Purpose; nay, to Reason its self; for who knows,
but under the Colour of an Opera, they may sing Mass as they
have done before; witness, *A Hymn to the Virgin*, written by Cardinal Coscia, and sung by *Signora Catsoni* to a Harp, etc. in the Opera
of *Julius Cæsar*, the words are these:

> V'adoro Pupille
> Saete D'amore
> Le vostre faville
> Son Grato nel Sen.

> Pietoso vi brama
> Il mesto mio Core
> Ch'ogn' ora vi chiama
> L'amato suo ben.

"*In English thus*, I worship thee, O Holy Virgin, Perfection of
Divine Love, thy Sacred Influence fills my Soul with Comfort.
My contrite Heart piously burns with fervent Desire towards
thee, while my glad Tongue is ever singing forth thy Praise: O
lovely and beloved Virgin, Author and Centre of my Happiness."

Except for slight errors the Italian text of the aria is given as
sung in Act II by Cuzzoni as Cleopatra, in 1724, with Senesino
in the cast as Giulio Cesare. The Opera was revived in 1725,
1730 and 1732 with Senesino, but in 1730 and 1732, Signora
Strada sang in place of Cuzzoni, who had left London for Vienna.

The English version "I worship thee", etc. as given in the
pamphlet is however an invention of the author, the original of
which in the 1724 libretto by N. F. Haym reads:

> Your charming Eyes my ravish'd Soul adores,
> The thrilling Pain my Heart with Pleasure bears;
> When you with Pity look my Sorrows cease;
> For you alone can heal the Wounds you gave.

The pamphlet is more fully described by me in *The Music Review*,
May 1964, pp. 114–19.

These examples of some of my fortunate finds will probably encourage others to go on looking for something new to turn up about Handel's works.

19

PORTRAITS, STATUES, SCULPTURES, ETC., OF HANDEL

HANDEL WAS A popular subject for the painters and sculptors of his time, as is obvious from Dr. J. M. Coopersmith's "A List of Portraits, Sculptures etc. of Georg Friedrich Händel", (*Music and Letters*, Vol. XIII, No. 2, April 1932, pp. 156–67). This excellent article, which naturally requires supplementing and some correction, lists forty-nine original paintings, fourteen sculptures, fourteen miniatures, and a long list of prints, engravings, caricatures, etc. An earlier less ambitious work was by R. A. M. Stevenson: "Handel and his Portraits" and appeared in *The Magazine of Art*, Vol. VIII, pp. 309–16 (Cassell & Co., London, 1885). "Some Handel Portraits reconsidered" is included in *Concerning Handel*, pp. 111–42 (Cassell & Co., London, 1948). W. S. Rockstro in his *Life of George Frederick Handel*, 1883 (Chap. XLIV) gives valuable information on the portraits, the Will, manuscripts and other personal effects of the composer. Innumerable articles and reproductions of portraits have been published from time to time which cannot be listed here, neither is it necessary to mention the artists named by Coopersmith except to comment on the fact that he includes seventeen oil paintings by Thomas Hudson, which suggests that some of them may be copies or inaccurately described.

Louis François Roubiliac, the famous eighteenth-century sculptor, who worked in London has nine statues, busts or monuments to his credit in Coopersmith.

Handelians are familiar with the Houbraken engraving that

figures so frequently in the large scores of Handel's oratorios published by William Randall from 1768 onwards. This was supposed to be based on a portrait, now in the National Portrait Gallery, by Francis Kyte, painted in 1742. I was able to discover and establish the fact that the Houbraken was first engraved and given away with Walsh's score of *Alexander's Feast* in 1738, and that therefore the Kyte and other copies were based on the Houbraken. The whole story is fully told in *Concerning Handel*. In June 1947, a portrait in oil came up for sale at Sotheby's listed as the Kyte. This however was incorrect. It is a copy of the Kyte with the addition of an open score of *Messiah* in front of Handel, and is now in my collection.

I concluded the article in *Concerning Handel:*

> "Although there still remain a number of unanswered questions about the origin of the Houbraken engraving and the Kyte painting, some previously accepted statements and conclusions have now been corrected; and it is hoped that the study of a rather baffling Handel problem may encourage further investigation and lead to the discovery of other portraits of the composer, including perhaps, an original painting from which the Houbraken was taken."

To my surprise and delight important information came from South Africa, in a letter to Julian Herbage in August 1959 from a Mr. Gordon R. Small of Pietermaritzburg, Natal, saying that he had bought a rather damaged oil painting, of which he enclosed a photograph, and suggested that it was a copy of the original oil painting from which the engraver had prepared the Houbraken frontispiece reproduced in Herbage's *Messiah*, p. 51 (Max Parrish, London, 1948). Julian Herbage kindly passed the letter and photograph to me to answer. I therefore wrote to Mr. Small for further information and a full face photograph – the other having been taken at an angle. I agreed to write up the matter for the Press and that my short article with reproduction of the picture should appear in *The Musical Times*. I have no doubt that, whether this portrait is the original from which Houbraken did his engraving or not, it is certainly connected with the subject, and a very interesting find. (See *The Musical Times*, April, 1963.)

There is a Handel portrait in the possession of the Shaftesbury family at St. Giles about which Betty Matthews has published an article with reproduction of the portrait in *Music and Letters*, January, 1963, pp. 43–45. In this the writer says that the portrait is signed on the back: "A portrait of Handel by Susan, Countess of Shaftesbury, done at St. Giles where he was often resident". The portrait has similarities with the Houbraken and Kyte portraits, and on the problem of origin Betty Matthews suggests that it is likely that it is a copy of the Kyte, although she had no clear evidence to that effect. It is however one more interesting link in the chain of Handel portraits of the period.

How many Handelians know that on the premises of Messrs. Novello & Co., 160 Wardour Street could be seen the Roubiliac statue of Handel,[1] the successful execution of which, according to Horace Walpole, laid the foundation of the artist's well merited success. The statue, completed in 1738, for which Roubiliac received £300, was commissioned by Jonathan Tyers, the owner of Vauxhall Gardens, where it was placed. Various contemporary prints show it in different parts of the Gardens. I am fortunate enough to own an exceedingly rare pamphlet giving the whole story – description and history of the statue from 1738 until it was acquired by the Sacred Harmonic Society in June 1854.[2] When the Society was disbanded in 1882 the statue was purchased by Mr. Henry Littleton of Novello & Co.[3] A fine reproduction of it appeared in *The Musical Times*, December 14, 1893 (special Handel number) of which Novello's have frequently issued copies. The statue was removed from Vauxhall Gardens in 1818 by the Rev. Jonathan Tyers Barrett, who had succeeded to the property but felt that it was inconsistent with his sacred profession. It was offered to public auction by Messrs. Robins,

[1] Now in the Victoria and Albert Museum.
[2] *Remarks on Roubiliac's Statue of Handel*, J. F. Puttick, London, 1855.
[3] *The Musical Times*, December 14, 1893, p. 27. "The Life of George Frederick Handel", W. S. Rockstro, Macmillan & Co., London, 1883, pp. 210–11.

9

April 11, 1818. Robins acquired the statue and removed it to his own residence, Duke St., Westminster. In 1830 it was offered for sale by Mr. Christie and fetched £210. On March 16, 1833 it was offered for sale by Mr. Squibb of Savile Row, when Mr. Brown, of University St. bought it for £215 5s. od, who sold it to the Sacred Harmonic Society for 100 guineas, as stated, in June 1854. Such are some of the details as they appear in Puttick's pamphlet. The original terra cotta model for the statue by Roubiliac is in the Fitzwilliam Museum.[1]

Roubiliac, as is generally known, was responsible for the Handel Monument in Westminster Abbey, one or two busts, and the death mask of the composer. Gerald Coke owns one of the terra cotta models by Roubiliac for the monument in Westminster Abbey.

The following notice of an unidentified bust of Handel appeared in the *Public Advertiser*, April 19, 1758:

> "To the Lovers of Music, particularly those who admire the Compositions of Geo. Frederick Handel, Esq.; F. Bull, at the White Horse, on Ludgate Hill, London, having at a great expence procured a fine Model of a Busto of Mr. Handel, proposes to sell by Subscription thirty Casts in Plaister of Paris. The Subscription Money, which is to be paid at the Time of subscribing, and for which a Receipt will be given, is one Guinea, and the Casts, in the order in which they are finished, will be deliver'd in the Order in which the Subscriptions are made. The Busto, which will make a rich and elegant Piece of Furniture, is to be twenty-three Inches and a half high, and eighteen Inches broad. The model may be viewed till Monday next, at the Place above mentioned", etc.

It would be interesting to know whether examples of this bust exist today, and if they are related to any of the Roubiliac's (genuine or reputed). The measurements given should make identification fairly certain.

(Extract from "More Handeliana", *Music and Letters*, January 1953, p. 23.)

[1] *Deutsch. Handel. A documentary biography*. Illustration facing p. 480.

Perhaps the best known statue of Handel is that in the Markt-platz, Halle, East Germany, round which Handelians from many countries have been accustomed to celebrate and honour the master over the years since its erection in 1859. I have been a privileged and honoured guest at the Halle Handel Festivals from 1955 onwards, and with other English visitors have paid tribute and shared in the wreath laying and the attendant cele-brations. As the special number of *The Musical Times*, December 14, 1893 says:

> "The Statue in the Market-Place at Halle was erected to com-memorate the Handel Centenary (1859), in December 1857. The cost of it was raised by subscriptions from England and Germany, and it was mainly due to the enthusiastic labours of Jenny Lind (Madame Goldschmidt) that the efforts to do honour to the master in his native town were crowned with success. On the day of the unveiling of the monument a performance of *The Messiah* was given in the large Market Church, under the direction of Robert Franz, with Ferdinand David as leader of the violins, and the principal soprano was Jenny Lind herself. It is pleasant to note that the face of St. Cecilia which adorns the monument is a likeness of the distinguished singer. The statue, considerably larger than life, is cast in bronze and was the work of Professor (Hermann) Heidel, of Berlin."

This account does not appear to be quite accurate. It was on December 15, 1857 that Jenny Lind performed in *Messiah* there and the consecration (unveiling) of the statue was on July 1, 1859, with Robert Franz in charge of the musical programme, which included a performance of *Samson* in the Marktkirche.

An interesting letter appealing for support for the erection of the Statue appeared in *The Musical Times*, April 1, 1858, from Robert Bowley, Treasurer of the Sacred Harmonic Society, in the course of which he said:

> "Considerable progress has been made in the work, which it is intended shall be completed in the coming year, 1859 ... Her Majesty the Queen has been pleased to subscribe fifty pounds, and His Royal Highness the Prince Consort twenty-five pounds, to the fund raising in London ... the Members of the Sacred

Harmonic Society . . . on the 9th instant, voted Fifty Pounds towards the same object. The Committee of the Society have likewise forwarded to Berlin, for the use of the sculptor commissioned to execute the work, a cast from the face of the Statue of Handel by Roubiliac, now in the Society's Offices at Exeter Hall.

"Notwithstanding, however, the important assistance afforded by the Subscribers alluded to, the entire contributions from England do not much exceed £200, received from less than one hundred subscribers. . . .

"The object more especially in view being to elicit an expression of feeling from such a vast number of persons as would bear some fair proportion to the estimation in which Handel's genius is regarded in England, it will afford the Committee much pleasure (while not absolutely limiting the amount from Societies or individuals) to receive from you *and your friends* the small subscription of One Shilling each. . . .

"Although the sums raised in England are not to be forwarded until the Statue is in course of erection at Halle, it is most important that the amount available should be *at once* ascertained," etc.

I have no record of the total amount contributed as a result of this appeal. Fortunately the Statue escaped damage during the war, although the area was bombed.

An illustration from a wood-cut of the unveiling ceremony on July 1, 1859 is in Konrad Sasse's *Das Händel-Haus in Halle*, (Halle, 1958), together with a photograph of the gathering round the Statue at the Handel Festival in 1958, and one at the time of the 1961 celebrations appeared in *The Musical Times*, August 1961. The iron railings shown round the statue in *The Musical Times*, December 14, 1893 were an addition to the original erection and were subsequently removed. The *Hallesches Monatsheft*, No. 4, July 1954 contains an informative article, "Das Händel-denkmal in Halle (Saale)", by Werner Piechocki.

The Händel-Haus in Halle contains a great many pictures, engravings, busts, medals, etc. of Handel and his contemporaries, including fifty-eight portraits of the composer all reproduced in the attractive "*Katalog zu den Sammlungen des Händel-Hauses in Halle. 2 Teil. Bildsammlung, Porträts".* Halle an der Saale,. 1962 *(Porträtkatalog des Händel-Hauses)* which has a foreword by Konrad Sasse, director of the Händel-Haus.

The Robbins Music Portrait Collection, Fulham, London, in the possession of Eduard R. Robbins contains a large number of engravings, prints, reproductions, of portraits of Handel, his friends, associates, contemporaries, the theatres and other Handeliana. No catalogue is available, but a comprehensive work on the collections is in preparation.

The British Museum, The National Portrait Gallery, The Fitzwilliam Museum and other public institutions, Gerald Coke, Dr. James S. Hall and myself have collections of Handel portraits, engravings, etc., details of which cannot be included here. Further information on material about the portraits, sculptures, etc. is given in the *Händel-Jahrbuch VI. Jahrgang* 1933 (Breitkopf & Härtel, Leipzig), pp. 23–25; *Händel-Jahrbuch I. (VII.) Jahrgang* 1955 (Deutscher Verlag für Musik, Leipzig), and in the comprehensive bibliography of Handel by Konrad Sasse, published by VEB Deutscher Verlag für Musik, Leipzig 1963. This includes post war publications in East Germany, where a comprehensive work, *Georg Friedrich Händel. Persönlichkeit-Umvelt-Vermächtnis* (A Biography in Pictures), by Werner Rackwitz and Helmut Steffens was published by VEB Deutscher Verlag für Musik, Leipzig, 1962.

The article, "Gustav Waltz: was he Handel's Cook?" *(Concerning Handel*, pp. 165–94) has as illustration the portrait attributed to F. L. Hauck. Another portrait painted by John Michael Williams, formerly in the possession of the late Arthur Hill, and now in the Royal College of Music, is reproduced in the 1959 edition of Newman Flower's *Handel*. On November 26, 1958, Sotheby's sold for £2,050 a "Portrait of a Musician" by Cornelius Troost (of Amsterdam), signed and dated 1736 on panel. There is no doubt in my mind that this is a portrait of Waltz, who therefore may have been of Dutch origin.

20

HANDEL FESTIVALS AND OPERAS
IN GERMANY FROM 1920–62

WHY THE ITALIAN OPERAS of Handel appeared to die almost at birth is a problem not to be settled here. Even in Germany, which had an early acquaintance with some of them in Hamburg from 1715 to 1734, after their production in London, the works were not kept alive. The few occasional performances here and there in Germany in the nineteenth century created no tradition for them and, as has been stated the English revival of them got off to a slow start in the 1930's, but is now likely to find increasing support for regular performances under one direction or another. The German Renaissance began in Göttingen with performances of *Rodelinde*, June 26, 28, 29, 1920 and has continued to the present day in connection with the Göttingen Handel Festivals, which have inspired performances elsewhere in Germany, particularly at Halle (Saale), where a Festival was staged in May 1922, that attracted a number of English guests including Newman Flower. Among other works the opera *Orlando Furioso* was performed, and the oratorios *Semele* and *Susanna*.

Informative articles on the Festivals and operas in Germany are:

Die neue Händel-Opern-Bewegung. Rudolf Steglich. (*Händel-Jahrbuch* . . . I. Jahrgang 1928, Breitkopf & Härtel, Leipzig, pp. 71–158.)

Die Göttinger Händel Festspiele. Festschrift. Göttingen, 1953.

Chronik der Göttinger Händelfestspiele nach 1953. (*Göttinger Händelfestspiele* 1959, Göttingen, pp. 44–5.)

Verzeichnis des Schrifttums über Georg Friedrich Händel. Kurt Taut. (*Händel-Jahrbuch* . . . VI. Jahrgang 1933. Breitkopf & Härtel, Leipzig, pp. 146–7.)

Verzeichnis des Schrifttums über Georg Friedrich Händel für die Jahre 1933–1954. Konrad Sasse. (*Händel-Jahrbuch* I. (VII.) Jahrgang 1955. Deutscher Verlag für Musik, Leipzig, pp. 105–138.)
Die Göttinger Händelopern-Renaissance I. Von 1920 bis 1934. Rudolf Steglich. II. 1934–1953. Uwe Martin. (*Musica*, 1956. Heft 9, pp. 585–91. Bärenreiter-Verlag, Kassel und Basel.)
Die Göttinger Händel-Bewegung. Heinz Ronte. (*Musica*, 1959, pp. 15–19. Bärenreiter-Verlag, Kassel und Basel.)

Of these the first work by Rudolf Steglich is most comprehensive and includes a table: "Übersicht über die szenischen Händel-Aufführung vom Sommer 1920 bis Sommer 1927". This records performances of *Admet, Ariodante, Ezio, Julius Cäsar, Orlandos Liebeswahn, Otto und Theophano, Radamisto, Rodelinde, Siroë, Tamerlan* and *Xerxes*, in Göttingen, Halle, Berlin, Bremen, Bremerhaven, Essen, Kassel, Hanover and many other places. The footnote to the table gives *Julius Cäsar*, 222 performances; *Rodelinde*, 136 performances; *Xerxes*, 87 performances; *Otto und Theophano*, 51 performances – a considerable record when compared with that of this country. The Göttingen performances are comprehensively treated in detail in the attractive *Die Göttinger Händel-Festspiele. Festschrift*, Göttingen, 1953, which is admirably illustrated. It is unnecessary therefore to deal with the performances more fully here or attempt an account of their excellence.

Herr Landgerichtspräsident i. R. Walter Meyerhoff, who I frequently met in Halle, invited me to the Göttingen Handel Festival from June 27 to July 5, 1959. He is the enthusiastic organizing head of these Festivals, which have gone on uninterruptedly (as stated) since 1920. The highlights of the year I attended were performances of *Ariodante*, which I was able to compare with the Halle version of the opera given in April 1959, and most interesting stage performances of *Belshazzar* in the Johanneskirche, with Rolf Apreck and Günther Leib from Halle in the cast – a very impressive production. The programme includes an illuminating and scholarly article on "Händels Belsazar" by Ludwig Finscher showing the very original stage setting, and among other items a short contribution by me: "Die Händel-Tradition und -Pflege in England. Eine geschichtliche Untersuchung" ("Handel Tradition and Practice in England. A Historical Review"). The Göttingen Festival was a fascinating experience and I have regretted that I have not been able to accept the kind invitations to attend subsequent Festivals which I have had from President Meyerhoff.

The Halle Handel Festival of May 25–28, 1922, which Newman Flower attended, was reported on by E. van der Straeten in *The Musical Times*, July 1, 1922.

The next Festival was in 1929, when *Julius Cæsar* and *Frohsinn und Schwermut* (*L'Allegro ed il Penseroso*) were given.

In 1930 there was established at Halle the Anglo-German Cultural Exchange (Deutsch-Englische Kulturaustausch), the founder of which was Dr. Lore Liebenam, and this Society, with the co-operation of the Halle musical authorities and the University launched an ambitious Festival in February 1935. The programmes included: *Semele, Susanna, Orlando Furioso,* (*Orlandos Liebeswahn*), *Messiah, Partenope, Tamerlane,* extracts from *Alcina, The Water Music,* the solo cantata, *Lucrezia,* and instrumental works, etc.

This Festival created a great interest in Germany and abroad and is of special significance in view of the modern East German Communist interpretation of Handel's life and work, which is directly opposed to the political twist given to the 1935 Festival. There, on February 22 Alfred Rosenberg, a prominent Nazi, afterwards tried at Nuremberg, and executed, made a speech in which he presented Handel as a German Viking, an example of the Master Race, according to Richard Capell who was present on the occasion and who wrote a full report of the Festival in the *Daily Telegraph*, March 2, 1935, which commenced:

> "Romain Rolland should have been at Halle last week-end to add his version of Handel's character and career to the various interpretations offered at the anniversary celebrations. Rolland's Handel – his head bloody but unbowed, a Promethean artist tormented by Philistine vultures – would have made an interesting

third to set alongside Alfred Rosenberg's Handel – a German Viking – and Edward Dent's man of fashion, a Handel moving as to manner born amid the Queen Anne furniture and the aristocracy of the London of 'The Rape of the Lock'."

Here is a translation of extracts from Rosenberg's speech:

"George Frederick Handel followed an eventful course, travelling from his home far and wide across the European countries. He felt the artistic heartbeat of their peoples, measured himself against them and their art forms, in order to express them in all spheres according to his nature, And this, his nature – we may certainly state this now – was not characterized by sweetly pious devotion, but by a strong dramatic sense, which repeatedly comes into prominence; in the heroic wrestling of all the elements of a turbulent humanity, compared with which the titles and texts of his works mean little . . ."

"The Messiah of Judaism and Handel's *Messiah* have in the last analysis inwardly nothing in common. This was probably already felt by his contemporaries, who often called him 'the great pagan'. The mighty fanfares of this work are a victory jubilation, delighting in struggle, which will always be understood by the European mind, whether in England or Germany. Even the representation of humble contrition, as apparently expressed in the text, is musically interpreted by Handel in a way full of vigour and prepared for defence . . ."

"It was the whole might of this man, whom we are honouring today, which impressed Beethoven in a brotherly, related way. That is why today, in a time of great conflict, our experience of Handel is quite different from that of a pious, or sweetly romantic epoch. Wide circles of the German people knew of Handel only as the exponent of weakly pious music, or entirely as interpreter of opinions expressed in the Old Testament. Because of a few sacred works which are performed again and again, one forgets the gigantic extent of his creative achievements, of all the glittering operas and powerful instrumental works. It was overlooked that behind these creations there stood not a feeble soul, but a great passionate personality, showing itself inwardly as well as outwardly."[1]

[1] Georg Friedrich Händel. Rede . . . am 22 Februar 1935 in Halle. Georg Kallmeyer Verlag. Wolfenbüttel und Berlin. 1937. For German text, see pp. 154-5.

Professor E. J. Dent in a speech at Halle on February 24, 1935, said in German of Handel's oratorio period:

"The oratorios were written for an aristocratic audience – for an audience which would never have been satisfied with non-literary libretti. In Germany it is not well understood why he used so many stories from the Old Testament for this purpose. He chose them in the first place because they were dramatic, and also fairly familiar to the English audience – although the stories of *Judas Maccabæus* and *Alexander Balus* were less well known by English readers than those of *Semele* or *Hercules*. Also, it is a historical fact that English listeners would instinctively link the old Hebrews with the Protestant Church . . . .

"At that time England was a country of religious and political freedom. This explains why Handel liked living there and never returned to Germany, except on short visits. In Hanover, he would have been obliged to be the servant of a Prince, always under the burdensome pressure of a fussy court etiquette. Although in England, too, he was a court employee, the court of the German King in England was of less importance. Social contact was maintained with the court; the King was honoured because he was a King, and a protestant King at that; but English society led its own life, independent of the whims of its ruler. And Handel moved in this society not as a servant, but almost as an equal. . . .

"He had no feeling at all for the popular element in music, apart from short episodes in which momentarily he is looking for local exotic colour, as, for example, in the Pastoral Symphony in the *Messiah*. He never wrote for the people; indeed, he despised them, as we know from his own words. He composed his works for a noble, humanistically highly educated, aristocratic society. Among the great composers, Handel is the great aristocrat."[1]

Rolland's presentation of the composer's character and work occurs particularly in "A Portrait of Handel", Chapter III of *A Musical Tour through the Land of the Past* (Kegan Paul, French, Trubner & Co., London, 1922), and *Handel* (Second edition, Kegan Paul, French, Trubner & Co., London, 1920).

The East German post war Handelians make great use of

[1] Händel in England. Gedächtnis-Rede . . . in Halle am 24. Februar 1935. Max Niemeyer Verlag. Halle (Saale), 1936. For German text, see pp. 155-6.

Rolland as a justification of their political interpretation of Handel's work, a characteristic contribution to the subject being "Das Händelbild Romain Rollands", which occupies pp. 20–38 of Johanna Rudolph's *"Händelrenaissance" Band I*, Aufbau-Verlag, Berlin, 1960. It was also dealt with by Antonín Sychra in a speech at Halle in 1959. (*Konferenzbericht*, pp. 219–21.).[1] R. G. Lambert who was at the Festival in 1935 commented on the fact that a concert was "broken into two parts by long political-mystical-musical orations by Herr Rosenberg, Germany's cultural dictator, and other local Nazi leaders". (*Listener*, March 6, 1935.)

Writing of this Festival in the *Observer*, March 3, 1935, Newman Flower said:

"There is one story which I believe has not been told. After the performance of Handel's (*Ode for*) *St. Cecilia* – a beautiful rendering which would have pleased the man who conceived it – we went to the Marktplatz. It was a clear night with cold stars in the sky and a bitter wind. Some thousands of people had gathered about the Handel statue to await the midnight hour which would bring in the two hundred and fiftieth birthday of Handel. Thirty-six uniformed youths held their blazing torches aloft about the statue. A hundred yards away the church where Handel had learned his first notes on the organ, stood out, a creation of white beauty in the floodlights. Musicians waited in the gallery between the spires to play to the waiting thousands when the midnight hour had struck. A black sea of people seemed to reach across the square to the steps of the church. There was no sound, no movement. But with midnight came a great clangour of bells. Presently the crowd began to shuffle and whisper. The vast human sea became restless. Hitler was expected. He would be here in five minutes. Hitler was asleep in the train which drew in to Halle at this very hour. Overworked and driven, he was sleeping on his journey from Berlin to Munich. Four officials of Halle went to the station to meet the train, to beg him to come – if only for ten minutes – to greet this city of Handel in her hour of celebrations. They were told that Hitler slept and must not be disturbed, and the train swept on into the night."

The programme of the 1935 Festival included major Handel

[1] Romain Rollands Händel-Bild heute gesehen.

works: *Cäcilien-Ode, Der Messias,* the opera *Otto und Theophano,* the "Orchesterkonzert Nr. 29" and other instrumental items. It is interesting to note in view of what happened at some of the Festivals after the war that there was a Festival Service "in der Kirche U.L. Frauen" (Marktkirche), and after the notice of *Messiah* in the programme was the following "Zu Ehren Händels wird das grosse Halleluja des 2. Teiles stehend angehört." Apparently the Nazis had not entirely broken with the tradition that *Messiah* was a religious work and Handel a Christian.

An exhibition was also arranged at the Moritzburg Museum in Halle from February 23 to April 14, 1935, a catalogue of which was issued: "*Händel Ausstellung anlässlich der 250. Wiederkehr des Geburtstages Georg Friedrich Händels,* Halle, 1935." Newman Flower and others lent exhibits, but in spite of interesting prints, drawings and literature, etc. the exhibition had little to offer in the way of printed or manuscript music by Handel, a deficiency which is still regrettable in the Handel House Museum at Halle to-day with its otherwise wide range of exhibits.

At the 1935 Festival

> "commemoration medals in silver were presented to Professor Dent (Cambridge), Professor Torrefranca (Milan), Mr. Stroud Read and Mr. Newman Flower, of London; and Mr. Melfort d'Alton, of Dublin. The company then witnessed the unveiling of a memorial tablet on the house where Handel was born and the opening of the Handel Exhibition in the Moritzburg." (*The Times,* February 25, 1935.)

This report is not quite accurate, the present Handel House is on the site of the house in which Handel was born.

In celebration of the two hundred and fiftieth anniversary of Handel's birth on February 23, 1685, the *Illustrirte Zeitung,* Nr. 46, February 14, 1935 contained a fully illustrated article, "Georg Friedrich Händels Leben und Werk", by Joseph Müller-Blattau, and a short article by Hans Schirmer, "In der Werkstatt der Händel-Renaissance. Ein Besuch bei Chrysander, dem Gärtner und Händelforscher". This has some interesting illustrations of Chrysander in his workshop, his primitive printing press, the workshop as a Museum and a photograph of his son Dr. Rudolph Chrysander.[1]

In 1942 the Nazis set about "Aryanizing Handel" by rewriting the text of the oratorios, *Judas Maccabæus* became *William of Nassau,* and the two collaborators, Klöcking and Harke, were entrusted with the still more difficult task of transforming *Israel in Egypt* into *Mongolesturm* (*Mongol Fury*). (*The Times,* February 16, 1942; *The Daily Telegraph,* February 11, 1942). *Judas Maccabæus* was also known as *Der Feldherr* (*Commander-in-Chief*) and the funeral anthem as *Helden Requiem* (*Heroic Requiem*).

It is as well to point out that elsewhere than in Germany Handel's works have been given a didactic interpretation not apparent in the works themselves but in the minds of those who wished to use them for ideological or political purposes. A corrupt version of *Belshazzar* was used in May 1938 when this work was staged as an opera for a week in London under the auspices of the Workers Music Association, with a large chorus from London Co-operative Societies, under the artistic direction of Alan Bush. H.W., in his report of this production in *The Musical Times,* June 1938, in which he praised some features of the performances, also said this:

> "Less defensible still was the revision of Jennens's libretto, which was altered, not always skilfully, with the apparent intention of pointing a more topical moral – that empires enslave and degrade and that the captive Israelites may be identified with the 'working classes'. Which was a mistake, for the sole and inescapable moral of the story is that the godless shall perish."

In April 1939 Alan Bush conducted another performance of *Belshazzar* at "The Festival of Music for the People", at the Albert Hall, and Richard Capell gave a long critical report of the performance in *The Daily Telegraph,* April 8, 1939, in which he dealt very fully with this version, by Randall Swingler, adapted to serve the purpose of a protest "against the iniquities of rampant

---

[1] See *Halle als Musikstadt,* Halle, 1954, for an article by Konrad Sasse: "Aus Halles Musikleben von der Mitte des 19 Jahrhunderts bis 1945", pp. 50–51 of which deal with the Festival and after, and pp. 53–71: "Der Aufschwung des hallischen Musiklebens seit 1945", by Professor Dr. Walther Siegmund-Schultze.

imperialism", and he quoted Jennens's text of the 1744 version of the chorus of Persians (No. 18) followed by Swingler's secularization of it.

Richard Capell also dealt with the use of the chorus, "O glorious prince", of which he said:

> "There was, however, a note in last Saturday's programme which cannot be acquitted of *suppressio veri*. It read: 'In one of Handel's greatest operas, *Belshazzar*, the final chorus depicts the dream of an international peace, brotherhood, and extended freedom, in such a stirring and convincing pattern that it was omitted from every performance until last year'." Capell continued: " 'O glorious prince' is in the first place not a dream, but a complimentary chorus addressed by the Persians to their general, Cyrus; nor is it the finale of the oratorio, which comes long afterwards in the form of the Chandos Anthem, 'I will magnify thee, O God'. It was rash, too, to assert that the long version of the chorus had never been sung before last year, seeing that it is nearly 100 years since Macfarren published it in the English Handel Society's edition of *Belshazzar*, as later Chrysander did in the German Handel Society's edition."

Capell's article deserves further quotations which cannot be given here. The whole subject could have been treated as past Handelian history not worth reviving, but for the facts that some East German producers and writers seem to have taken their cue from the distorted English version: have made it a bone of contention with the producers of the Göttingen Handel Festivals, and Bush himself in a speech at the Halle Festival in 1959[1] did a bit of special pleading for his interpretation of *Belshazzar*, hardly justified by the autograph manuscript, the earliest version and performances of the work, and the Novello (Macfarren) edition. It should be pointed out that Handel's first version (1745) of "O glorious Prince" consisted of only the first two lines of the chorus, the rest not being set by him until 1751, a fact which seems to have escaped Bush's and some East German writers' notice.

---

[1] *Händel-Ehrung der D.D.R. Konferenz Bericht*, 1959, pp. 257–60: 'Zum Problem der Verbreitung von Händels Schaffen unter dem grossen Publikum, besonders bei den Arbeiten und Bauern, durch szenische Aufführungen seiner Oratorien.'

Although not directly connected with the Handel Festivals, one publication during the years 1928–33 was the result of the Handel Renaissance at that time: the *Händel-Jahrbuch*. "Im Auftrage der Händel-Gesellschaft, herausgegeben von Rudolf Steglich . . . Breitkopf & Härtel, Leipzig."

The origin of the Händel-Gesellschaft, which was responsible for the *Year Book* is given in the introduction to the first volume:

> "In the summer of 1925 the Handel Society was formed, based on a fresh recognition of the greatness and importance of Handel's art. As successor of that other German Handel Society which was founded long ago by Chrysander and Gervinus, but developed in a different age and from different circumstances, it considers its task to help again in the furtherance of the knowledge and the cultivation of the great master of Halle."[1]

The *Year Books* contain interesting and important articles, particularly the 1933 volume which is the comprehensive Bibliography of Handelian literature: "Verzeichnis des Schrifttums über Georg Friedrich Händel von Kurt Taut". This series of *Year Books* was continued in Halle from 1955 onwards, and additions to the 1933 Bibliography appeared in the 1955 issue.

Other Jahrbuch articles of special interest are:

Händels *Jupiter in Argos*, das Werk, das er nie aufführte. Newman Flower. This is not correct – it was performed at the King's Theatre, May 1, 1739. (*Jahrbuch*, 1928, pp. 60–67).

Die neue Händel-Opern-Bewegung. Rudolf Steglich. (*Jahrbuch* 1928, pp. 71–158 – referred to above, p. 135.)

Englische Einflüsse bei Händel. Edward J. Dent. (*Jahrbuch* 1929, pp. 1–12.)

Fortunato Santini als Sammler und Bearbeiter Händelscher Werke. Karl Gustav Fellerer. (*Jahrbuch* 1929, pp. 25–40.)

Studien zur Arientechnik in den Opern Händels. Bruno Flögel. (*Jahrbuch* 1929, pp. 50–156.)

Betrachtung des Händelschen *Messias*. Rudolf Steglich. (*Jahrbuch* 1931. pp. 15–78.)

Werke Händels in der Gräfl. von Schönbornschen Musikbibliothek. Fritz Zobeley. (*Jahrbuch* 1931, pp. 98–116.)

[1] For German text, see p. 156.

Die Händelaufnahmen im Wiener Meisterarchiv. Robert Haas.
(*Jahrbuch* 1931, pp. 117–126.)
Studien zu Händels *Alexanderfest*. Leo Schrade. (*Jahrbuch*
1932, pp. 38–114.)

The post war series of Halle Handel Festivals commenced in
1952, and have continued yearly up to the present time. I was
honoured to be a guest from 1955 onwards, and hope in due course
to publish a full scale account of them and of my experiences over
the years at Halle. Detailed description is therefore outside the
scope of the present work, but it may be of interest to mention
here some sources giving details of the programmes which will
serve as guides until the larger work on the subject appears.

The *Festschrift zür Händel-Ehrung der Deutschen Demokratischen
Republik*, 1959 (Deutscher Verlag für Musik, Leipzig, 1959)
contains comprehensive lists of the works performed (Handel
and other composers) at the Festivals 1952–58, and of the Handel
publications (including the *Festschriften* and *Jahrbücher*) 1952–59.
Reports of the Festivals by Dr. Hall, Norman Stone and myself
appeared in *Musical Opinion*, August 1955, October 1956,
September 1957 and June 1959, and in *The Musical Times*,
August 1956, August 1957, August 1958, June 1959, July 1960,
August 1961 and August 1962; and in *Opera*, Vol. 10, No. 7,
July 1959, by Julian Herbage ("Handel at Halle").

The Festivals were very well organized and guests from many
countries were warmly welcomed and treated with great hospitality. We could move about with ease and comfort. In addition
to the illuminating musical experiences it was of great interest
to me personally to learn at first hand much of what was going
on behind the Iron Curtain, where I made many friends and
greatly enlarged my knowledge of Handel. I was able to hear
sixteen operas, over twenty oratorios and choral works besides
much of the church and instrumental music of the composer,
in addition to a great many items by classical and present day
composers both of the East and the West. The Festivals were
sponsored and financially supported by the State and the City

authorities of Halle; choirs and orchestras from different cities taking part. The production, interpretation and performance of the works were of the highest order, the Halle Opera Company being a permanent body with all the advantages of its own conductor, orchestra, producers, scenic artists and singers. The staging and acting were very convincing and the orchestral playing of rare quality and dramatic interpretation. Handel is truly being honoured to-day by the Festivals in the city of his birth.

21

HANDEL'S CHARACTER – SPEECHES
IN HALLE – CONCLUSION

SO MUCH HAS BEEN SAID and written about Handel's character and work that further comment by me may seem superfluous. But in view of the modern tendency of some writers here, and more particularly of those in East Germany to-day, to present an entirely new picture of Handel, to that in all the early records that we have of him, I may be excused for expressing some personal opinions. These are extracts from one or two of the many speeches I was asked to make in Halle during the Handel Festivals from 1955 onwards:

"As I stand here in the Market Place within a stone's throw of the spot where he was born, looking up at the great towers of the Church where he climbed the steps to Zachow at the organ, I think of him as a boy like most boys, fond of his home, his friends and his games, and I see as it were the beginning of that road on which he set his feet with conviction and determination and which he trod with ever growing success in his musical achievements, and increasing honour among men.

"As I read everything I can about his life's journey and his artistic expression, I find the story of one who with steadfastness of purpose, not baffled by temporary difficulties, gave himself to the task of fulfilling his musical destiny. The clarity, melody and harmony found in his music are as it were echoes of those things in his personality, and it is right that as we delight in his music we should honour the man. Hero worship can be overdone, but there are some figures in history who stand out so clearly for their over all greatness, that they compel unusual admiration. And Handel was indeed one of these exceptional men.

"I think he lived happily with his friends and associates of the Church, the Court, the Theatre, and among the common people. And as he seemed to be at home in Hamburg, in Italy, in Hanover and in England he must have had a simple graciousness which made him welcome everywhere.

"It is dangerous sometimes to try and interpret an artist's character and philosophy from his work. But as we come to know more of Handel's music and more about the facts of his life, they both appear to be the expressions of a sane and balanced man – capable, shrewd, honest and dependable. His genius is without question; not that he departed a great deal from the musical tradition and convention that he inherited, but in all that he did there is the sure touch of the experienced craftsman and the personal illumination of the inspired artist.

"Some music appeals to people of all races, ranks and creeds, and this is especially true of most of the music of Handel. It explains the presence here of those of us who have come from other lands. It is a challenge to all of us to strengthen the bonds of human understanding, confidence and friendship." (1957)

"I wonder who if any of the composers of to-day will be remembered 200 years from now – supposing mankind finds some way to preserve his existence until then. There must be some obvious reasons why the music of Handel, or at least some of it, is known and loved throughout the world to-day. Nothing can give permanence to the poor and trivial in art, and any attempt to force upon mankind false values, and to demand admiration for transitory works is doomed to failure in the end. The seeds of permanence or decay are in the works themselves – not in what we think about them. We must remember too that often great musical works cannot easily be analysed. And however interesting it may be in some cases to pick them to pieces as it were, it is often best just to submit oneself to them, to allow the magic and mystery of their beauty and emotional influence to overwhelm us, to soak into our consciousness, to lift us up out of and above the material problems of our own lives and inspire us to noble purpose. It is true that the great composers and artists must speak out of their own experience, their own day and generation, and must to an extent reflect their own national spirit and characteristics, but these are not the things which make them great – indeed they may limit their full expression, although adding some qualities to their work. And frequently it is easy to emphasize these temporary and local influences out of all proportion to the larger qualities of the composer's genius.

"As Handel moved from Halle to Hamburg, to Italy, to England, he assimilated in turn from the peoples he mixed with, and gave to them all something from himself which was not only his or theirs but ours and the world's." (1958)

"The last eight years that I have been coming here have taught me much about Handel's music which I should not have known otherwise. I have made many friends here and had opportunities to meet Handelians from other countries, and the interchange of ideas and information between us must, I am sure, lead to better knowledge, understanding and appreciation of Handel the Man and the Musician. He is too big a figure to be contained in a small sphere, or explained in a sentence or two of popular praise. We must go on endeavouring to get the best out of his work and life. He has never been dead in England, whatever you may have been told to the contrary, although we must admit that the British people have sadly neglected his operas and some other works until recently. But this is being rapidly changed, as those of you who heard our Handel Opera Society's production of *Rinaldo* last year under Charles Farncombe must admit. . . ."

"National figure as he was, first in your country and then in mine, his work extends beyond the bounds of any temporary local, personal or political interpretation, and in its essence has a message of happiness, inspiration and hope for people of all classes who perform or listen to it." (1962)

"Much has been done in recent years to throw new light on Handel's music and how it was and should be performed, and an immense amount of literature on the composers's life, work and character has been turned out. But we must be very careful not to assume or pretend that we have rediscovered Handel. He was never lost – the essential features of his music and the clear lines of his strong character have been known to Handelians for more than 200 years. We are in danger of lifting him out of his century and circumstances in our modern attempts to understand and interpret him.

"Nothing of major importance has been added to the portrait of him as a man that was not known to his contemporaries and the early writers about him. Although details have been added or corrected the true picture of Handel is very much as recorded for us by Mainwaring, Burney, Hawkins, Schœlcher, Chrysander, Rockstro, and in the diaries, journals and letters of the time.

"I should like to quote from a letter to Dr. Burney from Lord Mornington, March 30, 1776, in the possession of Gerald Coke: ' . . . pray what idea am I to form of the new oratorios that are springing up every day. *The King of Harmony died when Handel died, We shall never have such choruss musick again*. I remember to have heard from a Lady the following anecdote of him. She being very musical, was invited by him to a private Rehearsal of the Messiah, and being struck with the Exceeding dignity of expression in the Chorusses, and other parts of ye oratorio so inimitably sett to the sacred words, after the musick was over she asked him how it was possible for him *who understood the English Language but imperfectly*, to enter so fully into the sublime spirit of the Words. His Answer is I think a Lesson to all Composers, at least of Sacred Musick. *Madam, I thank God I have a little Religion*. And certainly if a composer does not in some measure feel the passion he means to express, why his musick *cannot have expression in it*'."

"Omitting references to Handel's character from Burney, Hawkins and others, I will quote a letter which James Smyth, a great friend of Handel's wrote to Bernard Granville three days after the composer's death:

'Dear Sir,

'According to your request to me when you left London, that I would let you know when our good friend departed this life, *on Saturday last at 8 o'clock in the morn died the great and good Mr. Handel*. He was sensible to the last moment; made a codicil to his will on Tuesday, ordered to be buried privately in Westminster Abbey, and a monument not to exceed £600 for him. I had the pleasure to reconcile him to his old friends; he saw them and forgave them, and let all their legacies stand! In the codicil he left many legacies to his friends, and among the rest he left me £500, and has left to you the two pictures *you formerly gave him*. He took leave of all his friends on Friday morning, and desired to see nobody but the Doctor and Apothecary and myself. At 7 o'clock in the evening he took leave of me, and told me "we should meet again"; as soon as I was gone he told his servant "*not* to let me come to him any more for that he had *now done with the world*". He died as he lived – a good *Christian*, with a true sense of his duty to God and man, and in perfect charity with all the world. If there is anything that I can be of further service to you please to let me know. I was to have set out for Bath to-morrow but must attend the funeral, and shall then go next week. I am, dear Sir

Your most obedient humble servant,

James Smyth'."[1]

"Among the 30 or so of Handel's letters which are mostly factual with regard to his relatives, friends and work, there is no indication of introspection, speculation or philosophy.

"As we honour him to-day it is not only as a great musical genius but as a man with a simple faith which he learnt in his home and the Church in the Market Place here in Halle; as one who related his art to his life and his life to his art, both of which he used to serve the people of his day and generation, with a great heart, kindness, a love of children, generosity and practical charity." (Smith, *Handel's Life in England*. Speech. Halle. April 13, 1959. German text in *Konferenzbericht*, 1961, pp. 77–79. Deutscher Verlag für Musik, Leipzig.)

This is an inadequate story of Handel in my time so far. Many more people and works come into it than I have mentioned, but as such it does give, I hope, information and guidance to the reader or musician who may wish to consult some of the most important records of the composer's life and works, and what is being done to widen our knowledge of them. New biographies of Handel are a ceaseless stream, but it is doubtful, in spite of interesting new details that appear in some of them, whether

---

[1] *Mary Delany. Autobiography and Correspondence of Mary Granville*, 1861-2, Vol. III p. 549. *Deutsch. Handel. A documentary biography*, pp. 818–19.

much of importance has been added to what was known forty years or so ago. Handel told us very little about himself – it would be helpful if we had more of his letters, but unless some new hitherto unknown contemporary records come to light we must accept the picture of the man as we have it. What some of the musicians and musicologists have given us in recent years, are many serious attempts to perform and interpret the works from different points of view to those held more particularly in the last century and the early part of this. In carrying out this legitimate new approach it must be remembered that Handel was a man of his time, writing in the idiom of his time; accepting the philosophy and conventional Christian religion of his time. What he did was to touch everything he produced with his immortal genius. To lift his work out of the environment in which it arose, and to interpret it as that of a far-seeing humanist writing prophetically for modern Communist consumption is historical and technical nonsense, and unworthy of what is claimed as musical scholarship in this country, and more particularly behind the Iron Curtain.

What we want are still more performances of the lesser known works. Some thirty operas await modern stage production in this country, and many of the oratorios should be heard more often. To think of gems like *Il Parnasso in Festa* being quite unknown to English audiences, who are also ignorant of most of the hundred Italian cantatas; the twenty-two Italian duets, and much of the instrumental and harpsichord music, shows how much there is still to be done before Handel has been fully honoured in the country of his adoption.

APPENDIX

Books and articles by the same Author:

A Bibliography of the Musical Works published by John Walsh during the years 1695–1720. (Bibliographical Society, London, 1948.)

Concerning Handel: His Life and Works. (Cassell & Co. Ltd., London, 1948.)

Music Publishing in the British Isles from the Earliest Times to the Middle of the Nineteenth Century. By Charles Humphries and William C. Smith. (Cassell & Co. Ltd., London, 1954.)

The Italian Opera and Contemporary Ballet in London 1789–1820. (Society for Theatre Research, London, 1955.)

Handel. A Descriptive Catalogue of the Early Editions. By William C. Smith, assisted by Charles Humphries. (Cassell & Co. Ltd., London, 1960.)

Handel Catalogue. (*Grove's Dictionary of Music and Musicians.* Fifth edition. Vol. IV 1954, pp. 50–60.)

Catalogue of Works of Handel. (*Handel.* A Symposium edited by Gerald Abraham. O.U.P., London, 1954, pp. 275–310.)

Bibliographies to Newman Flower's *Biographies of Handel* (1923, 1947, 1959); *Sir Arthur Sullivan* by Herbert Sullivan and Newman Flower (with list of works, 1927, 1950); *Franz Schubert* (1928, 1949.) (Cassell & Co. Ltd., London.)

George III. Handel and Mainwaring. (*Musical Times*, September 1924.)

Footnotes to Musical History. (*Musical Times*, October 1924.)

The Earliest Editions of Handel's *Messiah*. (*Musical Times*, November 1925.)

Playford: Some hitherto unnoticed Catalogues of Early Music. (*Musical Times*, July, August 1926.)

Handel's First Visit to England. (*Musical Times*, March 1935.)

Handel's Birthplace. (*Musical Times*, April 1935.)

Handel's *Rinaldo*, An Outline of the Early Editions. (*Musical Times*, August 1935.)

Handel's First Song on the London Stage. (*Music and Letters*, October 1935.)

Handel's Failure in 1745. New Letters of the Composer. (*Musical Times*, July 1936.)

Recently Discovered Handel Manuscripts. (*Musical Times*, April 1937.)

Gustavus Waltz: Was he Handel's Cook? (*Musical Opinion*, December 1937; January, February, March, April 1938.)

Two Songs by Handel (from *Venus and Adonis*). (*British Museum Quarterly*, April 1938.)

Samson: the Earliest Editions and Handel's Use of the Dead March. (*Musical Times*, August 1938.)

The Earliest Editions of Handel's *Water Music*. (*Musical Quarterly*, New York, January 1939.)

Handel – The Man. (Land der Mitte-*Hallischen Nachrichten*, March 21, 1939; *Musical Opinion*, April 1939.)

Handel's *Messiah*: Recent Discoveries of Early Editions. (*Musical Times*, December 1941.)

The Harrow Replicas, Nos. 5–7. (*Musical Times*, May 1946.)

John Walsh: Music Publisher. (*The Library*, Fifth Series, Vol. I, No. 1, June 1946.)

Messiah. Julian Herbage. (*Music and Letters*, July 1948.)

Handel's *Messiah*. R. M. Myers. (*Music and Letters*, October 1948.)

Handel's *Messiah*. (*Radio Times*, December 17, 1948.)

Frank Kidson and his Work. (*Journal of the English Folk Dance and Song Society*, Vol. V, No. 3, December 1948.)

John Walsh and his Successors. (*The Library*, Fifth Series, Vol. III, No. 4, March 1949.)

Handeliana. (*Music and Letters*, April 1950.)

The Text of *Messiah*. (*Music and Letters*, October 1950.)

John Walsh, Music Publisher; His Opposition to the Duties on Paper, 1726 and 1734. (*Harvard Library Bulletin*, Vol. VI, No. 2, Spring 1952.)

The Meaning of the Imprint. (*The Library*, Fifth Series, Vol. III. No. 1, March 1952.)

More Handeliana. (*Music and Letters*, January 1953.)

A Catalogue of Music Published by John Walsh and his Successors, with a Preface by William C. Smith. (The First Edition Bookshop Limited, London, Catalogue No. 43, 1953.)

Wege zu Händel. (*Der Neue Weg*, Halle, June 1, 1957.)

Händels Stellung und Einfluss in England. (*Musica*, Bärenreiter, Kassel, January 1959.)

Handelian Research. (*Musical Times*, April 1959.)

Handel Festival at Göttingen. (*Musical Times*, September 1959.)

Die Händel-Tradition und -Pflege in England. (Göttinger Händelfestspiele 1959 Programme, Göttingen.)

Händels Leben in England – Unter besonderer Berücksichtigung seiner Blindheit. (Händel-Ehrung der Deutschen Demokratischen Republik. Konferenzbericht 1959. Deutscher Verlag für Musik, Leipzig, 1961.)

A Newly Discovered Handel Portrait. (*Musical Times*, April 1963.)

Do you know what you are about? A Rare Handelian Pamphlet. (*Music Review*, May 1964.)

"Adolf Hitler, The Founder of the Greater German Empire. One people we are – one Empire we shall be. As fanatically as we defend the greatness of this Empire, its peace, and also its honour, as little shall we tolerate any spirit of discord to endanger the unity of the nation, or ignorant selfishness to weaken the vigour of our political will – so much are we attached to the individual characteristics of the German countries, and we shall preserve the rich variety of our inner life." (*Land der Mitte*, March 21, 1939.)

See German text, p. 61.

"Georg Friedrich Händel hatte also einen schicksalsreichen Weg aus seiner Heimat weit über die Staaten Europas genommen. Er hat die künstlerische Seele der Völker schlagen gefühlt, sich mit ihr und ihren Kunstformen gemessen, um sie selbstherrlich auf allen Gebieten seinem Wesen gemäss zu gestalten. Und dieses sein Wesen, das können wir heute wohl sagen, war nicht süsslich fromme Hingebung, sondern ein immer wieder hervortretender starker dramatischer Anschlag, ein heroisches Ringen aller Elemente eines stürmenden Menschentums, dem gegenüber Titel und Texte seiner Werke nur wenig bedeuten" (p. 12).

"Der Messias des Judentums und der 'Messias' Georg Freidrich Händels haben innerlich letzlich nichts miteinander gemeinsam, was wohl schon seine Zeit empfand, die ihn öfters den 'grossen Heiden' nannte. Die gewaltigen Fanfaren dieses Werkes sind ein kampffroher Siegesjubel, den die europäische Seele, sei es in England, sei es in Deutschland, immer begreifen wird. Selbst die Darstellung demütiger Zerknirschung, wie sie in den Worten ausgedrückt erscheint, findet bei Händel eine kraftgesättigte, abwehrbereite musikalische Deutung" (p. 13).

"Die ganze Mächtigkeit des Mannes, den wir heute feiern, ist es gewesen, die auf Beethoven den brüderlich verwandten Eindruck gemacht hat. Darum erleben wir Händel heute in einer grossen kämpferischen Zeit auch ganz anders als eine pietistische oder süsslich romantische Epoche. In weitesten Kreisen des deutschen Volkes lebte nämlich Händel nur als ein Begriff schwächlicher, frömmelnder Musik oder gar als Deuter alttestamentlicher Gesinnung. Man vergisst über einzelne immer wieder dargestellte sakrale Werke das gigantische Ausmass dieses schöpferischen Gestaltens, all der glänzenden Opern und all seiner mächtigen Instrumentalwerke. Man übersah, dass hinter diesen Schöpfungen nicht eine schmächtige Seele stand, sondern eine gleich gross nach aussen wie nach innen ausströmende leidenschaftliche Persönlichkeit" (p. 8). (Alfred Rosenberg, *Georg Friedrich Händel*. Rede . . . am 22. Februar 1935 in Halle. Georg Kallmeyer Verlag. Wolfenbüttel und Berlin, 1937). For English translation, see p. 137.

"Die Oratorien sind für eine aristokratische Hörerschaft geschrieben, für eine Hörerschaft, die mit unliterarischen Texten nie zufrieden gewesen wäre. Man versteht nicht sehr gut in Deutschland, warum er so viele Geschichten aus dem Alten Testament zu diesem Zwecke verwendete. Er wählte sie erstens, weil sie dramatisch waren, und auch den Englischen Hörern ziemlich gut bekannt – obwohl die Geschichten von Judas Maccabäus und Alexander Balus dem englischen Leser viel weniger bekannt waren als jene von Semele oder Hercules. Dazu kam auch die historische Tatsache, dass englische Hörer instinktiv die alten Hebräer mit der protestantischen Kirche assoziierten" (pp. 13, 14).

"England war damals das Land der religiösen und politischen Freiheit; das erklärt uns, warum Händel gern dort lebte, warum er nie wieder (ausser zu kurzen Besuchen) nach Deutschland zurückkehrte. In Hannover hätte er Diener eines Fürsten sein

mussen, stets unter dem lästigen Druck einer kleinlichen Hof-
etikette. In England hatte er zwar eine Stellung am Hofe, aber der
Hof des deutschen Königs spielte in England keine führende
Rolle. Man verkehrte beim Hofe, man ehrte den König, weil er
König war, und ein protestantischer König; aber die englische
Gesellschaft lebte für sich, unabhängig von den Launen ihres
Herrschers. Und Händel verkehrte in dieser Gesellschaft nicht
als Diener, sondern fast auf gleichem Fusse" (pp. 14, 15).

"Für das Volkstümliche in der Musik hat er nicht das geringste
Gefühl, abgesehen von solchen kleinen Episoden, wobei er ganz
momentan ein exotisches Lokalkolorit sucht, wie z.B in der
Pastoralsymphonie des 'Messias'. Er hat nie für das Volk geschrieben; er verachtete das Volk, wie wir es aus seinem eigenen Munde
wissen. Er schrieb seine Werke für eine vornehme, humanistisch
hoch-kultivierte und aristokratische Gesellschaft; und unter all
den grossen Tondichtern ist Händel der grosse Aristokrat" (pp.
16, 17).

(Edward Dent. *Händel in England*. Gedächtnis-Rede . . . in Halle
am 24. Februar 1935.) For English translation, see p. 138.

"Aus einer neuen Erkenntnis der Grösse und der Bedeutung
der Kunst Händels ist im Sommer 1925 die Händel-Gesellschaft
gegründet worden. Als Nachfolgerin jener deutschen Händel-
Gesellschaft, die einst Chrysander und Gervinus ins Leben riefen,
aber in anderer Zeit aus anderen Verhältnissen erwachsend, setzt
sie sich die Aufgabe, erneut für die Förderung der Kenntnis und
Pflege des grossen Hallischen Meisters zu wirken." (*Händel-
Jahrbuch*, 1928, p. III.)

For English translation, see p. 143.

ADDITIONAL NOTE

"The Great Mr. Handel", a film in Technicolor, had its première at the Leicester Square Theatre on September 22, 1942, followed by a successful run. Directed by Norman Walker, screenplay by L. Du Garde Peach, music from Handel arranged and conducted by Ernest Irving, with the London Philharmonic Orchestra, it starred Wilfred Lawson (Handel), Elizabeth Allan (Mrs. Cibber—Gladys Ripley, vocalist) and A. E. Matthews (Jennens). It had a good press and was reasonably true to the popular story of Handel's life, including some apocryphal incidents. I went to the première and enjoyed it very much. It is a pity that it has never been revived, as far as I know.

Handel: Works—Miscellaneous

Persons, Places, Societies
and Works by other Composers than Handel

Books, Pamphlets, Articles and Speeches